BUS. $\alpha / 95$

ENLIGHTENED ENTREPRENEURS

ENLIGHTENED ENTREPRENEURS

Ian Campbell Bradley

Weidenfeld and Nicolson · London

George Weidenfeld and Nicolson Ltd
91 Clapham High Street, London SW4 7TA

ISBN 0 297 79054 4

Printed in Greath Britain by
The Bath Press, Avon

CONTENTS

ILLUSTRATIONS

ILLUSTRATIONS

Carnegie's birthplace in Dunfermline (Andrew Carnegie Birthplace Museum)

Early American skyscraper (Andrew Carnegie Birthplace Museum)

George Cadbury (Cadbury Schweppes PLC)

Cadbury's Cocoa Essence advertisement (Cadbury Schweppes PLC)

Houses in Bournville (Bournville Village Trust – Archives)

Joseph Rowntree (Joseph Rowntree Memorial Trust)

Rowntree's Elect Cocoa advertisement (Rowntree Mackintosh PLC)

Girls assembling coronation tins at Rowntrees (Rowntree Mackintosh PLC)

Wartime Boots advertisement (The Boots Company PLC)

Jesse Boot (The Boots Company PLC)

Boot's shop at 16–18 Goosegate, Nottingham (The Boots Company PLC)

William Hesketh Lever (Unilever PLC)

Sunlight Soap advertisement (Unilever PLC)

Street scene in Port Sunlight village (Unilever PLC)

Horse-drawn cart used by Lever sales representatives (Unilever PLC)

ACKNOWLEDGEMENTS

I have received an enormous amount of help in the preparation of this volume. Caroline Bingham, historian of Royal Holloway College, generously shared her knowledge of Thomas Holloway with me, and Ron Davis showed me the interesting collection of Holloway memorabilia in the Egham Museum. Audrey Tattam took me on a conducted tour of her native Saltaire while Tony and Sarah Whiting provided excellent hospitality while I was visiting there. Stephen Best, the local studies librarian at Nottingham, proved to be a mine of information on Samuel Morley and was able to direct me to some press cuttings which illuminated aspects of his career of which I had only a sketchy knowledge. Michael Hopkins, the director of corporate affairs at the Nabisco Group, lent me a very useful book on Huntley & Palmers and Godfrey Omer-Parsons showed me the fascinating collection of material relating to the history of the company in Reading Museum. I also had a helpful correspondence with the historian of Huntley & Palmers, Anthony Corley of Reading University.

My research on Jeremiah James Colman was expertly guided by Reginald Butcher, the retired archivist at Colmans of Norwich, and Dr Rodney Cross from the company's administrative and public relations department. Jane Paterson of the Carnegie United Kingdom Trust supplied me with some useful information on Andrew Carnegie and Derrick Barclay very kindly opened the birthplace museum specially for me to look round. Francis Stanley, the archivist at Cadbury Schweppes, gave me a very interesting historical tour of the Bournville works and Sir Adrian Cadbury, the company chairman, kindly read through and commented on a draft of my chapter on George Cadbury. The same service was performed on my Rowntree chapter by Robin Guthrie, director of the Joseph Rowntree Memorial Trust. I was also greatly helped in my research on Rowntree by Mrs Elizabeth Jackson, the Trust's librarian.

Dr Stanley Chapman of Nottingham University kindly answered some queries that I put to him about the life of Jesse Boot and Miss J.M. Leverton, chief assistant librarian in the industrial division of Boots in Nottingham, provided useful archival material on the history of the firm. Maureen Stanniforth and her excellent staff at the library at Unilever House and Ailsa Bowers at the Heritage Centre at Port Sunlight gave me enough William Lever material to fill an entire book, all of it fascinating!

To all of them I offer my sincere thanks for their time and patience. Also to my editor, Juliet Gardiner, to my parents who as always have had the daunting task of tidying up my grammar, and not least to my wife who has let me monopolize the new word processor that was supposed to be a joint toy. The gestation period of this book has almost exactly coincided with that of our first-born. I dedicate it to her in the hope that she will one day enjoy seeing what her father was up to when she was kicking about in her mother's womb.

Introduction

In the first issue of his *Cocoa Works Magazine*, Joseph Rowntree wrote that his aim in life was that of 'combining social progress with commercial success'. This book is about ten remarkable Victorian industrialists who pursued those two goals with such single-minded energy and to such spectacular effect that we are still benefiting from both their enterprise and their enlightenment today. The businesses which they created a hundred years or more ago are for the most part still thriving and include some of the most successful companies in contemporary Britain. The ideas and practices which they developed in the field of employee welfare and worker participation have been widely taken up and constitute a model of good industrial relations which has never since been bettered. The philanthropic institutions and charitable trusts which they established continue to improve the quality of life of millions.

There can be few people whose lives have not been touched in some respect by at least one of these enlightened entrepreneurs. Even those who have never succumbed to the temptation of a bar of Cadbury's chocolate, a packet of Rowntree's fruit gums or a tin of Huntley & Palmers' biscuits must surely have ventured into Boots the chemists. Most households have a tin of Colman's mustard in the sideboard and a packet of Persil or one of the other Unilever detergents by the washing machine. Those who are graduates of Royal Holloway College, who have ever patronized the Old Vic Theatre in London, whose children watch *Sesame Street* on television, or who live in one of the garden cities influenced by model communities like Saltaire, have more

1

direct cause to be grateful for the practical vision and generosity which characterized this remarkable group of Victorians.

In an earlier age the word 'romance' was often used for accounts of the lives of great industrialists. It is certainly not an inappropriate term to describe the stories which will be told in the pages that follow. All of the men featured in this book came from comparatively humble origins, some of them from considerable poverty. Two of them left school at thirteen, the rest a year or so later and not one of them went to university. Instead, they started their careers as unskilled apprentices, six of them working behind the counters of their parents' shops. From these inauspicious beginnings they rose to become among the richest and most influential men of their generation, employing thousands of people and often taking a leading part in the nation's political life.

They achieved success in widely diverse fields and in many different ways, but common to all of them was an ability to seize on some relatively simple technique which had not been tried before and which brought spectacular results. In some cases it was the exploitation of a new raw material or product. Titus Salt owed his position as king of the West Riding worsted trade largely to his manufacture of fine cloth from the wool of the alpaca. George Cadbury and Joseph Rowntree established their dominant position in the confectionery industry by introducing a new pure chocolate which was not adulterated with starch and other additives. Andrew Carnegie became the richest man in the world by seeing the potential of a new material, steel, before anyone else in the United States. For others, mechanization in an industry previously dominated by hand-work was the key element in their success. Samuel Morley revolutionized the hosiery business by switching from domestic knitters to factory production and George Palmer introduced machinery into biscuit making. Others again made their breakthroughs in the fields of marketing and advertising. Jeremiah James Colman and William Hesketh Lever saw the vital importance of good packaging and of a strong brand image in an age which saw the rise of a mass consumer market. Thomas Holloway and Jesse Boot were both consummate salesmen who realized the enormous potential of advertising in the new medium of the cheap daily press.

There are several themes which recur in the chapters that follow. Relocation of business is one of the most striking – six of the entrepreneurs moved their workforce from cramped inner-city premises and established new factories in what would nowadays be called 'green field' sites. Concern for the overall welfare of employees is another common theme, if not quite universal. Andrew Carnegie could hardly be said to be a model enlightened employer and the evidence about Thomas Holloway's treatment of his workforce is too scanty for us to be able to pass judgement, but the other eight industrialists featured in this book showed an active and practical concern for their workers which was quite remarkable in its scope and which has been matched by few employers since. Among the tangible results of their efforts are the four model industrial communities of Saltaire, Bournville, New Earswick and Port Sunlight, which stand as attractive living memorials to the enlightened face of Victorian capitalism.

For employees of Salts, Cadburys, Rowntrees and Lever Brothers the firm was a provider not just of wages but of housing, health care, education, recreation and entertainment. In the evenings there were company-run night schools and debates, at weekends company-run concerts and dances to attend and company-owned allotments to till, and on bank holidays works outings to the seaside or the country. The total environment that these firms provided for their workers, and the extent to which leisure as well as working time centred around the factory, is strongly reminiscent of the atmosphere prevailing in many Japanese businesses today. It reflected an approach which is often described as paternalistic. To some extent, that is a fair description. The entrepreneurs in this book did have a fatherly attitude towards their employees, with both the beneficial and the harmful side-effects that such an outlook brings. They cared deeply for the welfare of their workers but they did also tend to believe in giving them what they thought was good for them rather than what they themselves might have wanted, and there was often a strongly autocratic streak in their make-up.

Yet paternalistic though they may have been in some respects, these enlightened entrepreneurs were in other ways very democratic and even egalitarian in their attitudes. They shared a strong distaste for the growing polarization of capital and labour which they rightly discerned as one of the most powerful and pernicious trends of their age. For them employers, managers, office staff and shop-floor workers were all partners together. This idea of partnership was in several cases put into practice through the introduction of profit-sharing and co-partnership schemes. More fundamentally, it showed itself in a refusal to be distanced from the lives of workers. One of the most striking characteristics of these industrialists, who were among the richest men of their age, is the simplicity of their own lives. With few exceptions, they lived in fairly modest houses, often within walking distance of their factories, and did not escape into large and secluded country estates. They also tended to shun social engagements and conspicuous expenditure, preferring to spend their money on others rather than on themselves.

The business of giving away money was a dominant occupation of all those featured in this book. For some, like Thomas Holloway and Jesse Boot, it was largely confined to the last years of their lives. For others, like Samuel Morley and George Cadbury, the calls of philanthropy were constant throughout their lives. George Palmer and Jeremiah Colman gave spontaneously, motivated by Christian compassion and charity, while Joseph Rowntree carefully set out his principles of giving in lengthy memoranda and Andrew Carnegie formulated an entire Gospel of Wealth. Thomas Holloway and Titus Salt concentrated their giving on one or two large projects, while Samuel Morley and William Lever spread their benevolence among a wide range of religious, political and other good causes. All of them found it considerably easier to make money than to give it away, yet they shared a conviction that they held their wealth as trustees and that it should be used for the good of the community as a whole.

Two belief systems, one political and the other religious,

4

underlay both their commercial enterprise and their philanthropic enlightenment. They were deeply imbued with the values of Victorian Liberalism and of Protestant Christianity. On the face of it, the former seems to have exerted the stronger hold. Nine of the ten were actively involved in Liberal Party politics in the latter part of the nineteenth century and there is evidence that the tenth, Thomas Holloway, was certainly a committed Liberal if not actually a party activist. Five became Liberal MPs and three more were chairmen of their local Liberal associations. Andrew Carnegie, whose residence in the United States made active involvement in British politics difficult, gave substantial sums of money to the British Liberal Party and spoke at Liberal gatherings during his visits to Scotland.

Victorian Liberalism stood for free trade, self-help, minimal government interference and internationalism – all values calculated to appeal to industrialists and employers. It also stood for generosity and tolerance, for democracy and popular representation and for radical social reform, carried out by public authorities if necessary but preferably by the spontaneous voluntary actions of individuals and communities. It stressed the moral responsibilities of those with wealth and power towards those without it and, while falling short of full-blooded socialism, it had a strongly redistributionist and egalitarian flavour. It was also pre-eminently an anti-class movement, drawing its support from across the social spectrum and appealing on the basis of its ideas and principles rather than because of any particular sectional interest. W. E. Gladstone, the great leader of the Liberal Party, made his political appeals to the masses rather than the classes. It was hardly surprising that Gladstone was hero-worshipped by several of the enlightened entrepreneurs and admired by all of them. As chancellor of the exchequer in the early 1850s and 1860s he had laid the foundations of the free market economy in which they flourished. He also reminded them of the heavy responsibilities and duties which their wealth and influence conferred.

It was a reminder that they hardly needed. For more powerful even than their Liberal principles were the promptings of their

Nonconformist consciences. Religion was the dominant force in their lives, and it was religion of a particular kind, the demanding, rigorous creed of Nonconformity. Only two were outside the Nonconformist fold – Thomas Holloway, who was a member of the Church of England, and Andrew Carnegie, who forsook the Swedenborgian faith of his father for a universalist philosophy which drew on several of the world's great faiths, and which seems to have played a major part in shaping his character and motivating his philanthropy. For the rest it is scarcely too much to claim religion as the moving force behind both their commercial enterprise and their enlightened beneficence.

The argument that certain values stressed in Protestant Christianity helped the development of capitalism in Western Europe, first put forward by Max Weber and extended by Richard Tawney, is well known. There is also considerable agreement among historians that the values associated particularly with the Nonconformist or Dissenting denominations in the nineteenth century played an important part in making Britain the pre-eminent industrial and commercial power in the world. Certainly there could hardly be better exemplars of those Protestant virtues than our ten enlightened entrepreneurs. They were methodical, regular and thrifty in their habits, relentless in their capacity for hard work and self-improvement and models of self-discipline and temperance in their personal lifestyles. Seven of them were complete teetotallers and the other three drank very little and very infrequently. Without exception, they went to bed and rose early and preferred wholesome and distinctly bracing physical exercise, in many cases involving early morning plunges into cold baths, to the more decadent pleasures of smoking, gambling, dinner parties or dances.

Yet although they were often extremely strict on themselves they were not puritanical killjoys who sought to condemn others to a drab life deprived of all pleasures. They were, on the contrary, cultivated and cultured men with an open-minded attitude and an interest in many artistic and political movements. They also had a deep warmth and compassion and a determination to improve the lives of their fellow men, and particularly of those

6

with whom they came into personal contact, not just physically but also culturally, socially and morally. Nonconformity may have helped to make them good businessmen but it also made them humane and concerned employers and generous philanthropists. The story of the Good Samaritan carried as important a message for them as the parable of the talents.

The particular industrialists whose stories are to be found here are just a few among the many with similar backgrounds and principles and often with scarcely less impressive achievements who turned Victorian Britain into the greatest industrial and trading nation in the world. Some of the others will receive a brief mention in the following pages and it is perhaps worth listing the more familiar names here, grouped according to their particular religious affiliation.

There are three Quakers among our ten enlightened entrepreneurs (George Palmer, George Cadbury and Joseph Rowntree) and it is the Society of Friends which easily heads the denominational league table of leading Victorian industrialists. As well as Joseph Fry, the third famous name in chocolate making, and William Jacob and John Carr of Peek Freans who were Huntley & Palmers' great rivals in the biscuit business, leading Quaker industrialists in the nineteenth century included John Horniman, the tea packer, Isaac and James Reckitt who built up the blue and starch business which later merged with Colmans, Cyrus and James Clark, the Somerset shoe manufacturers who were cousins of George Palmer, Bryant & May the match makers and Allen & Hanbury the chemists. Then there were the famous Quaker banking dynasties like the Lloyds, the Barclays, the Gurneys and the Peases, several of whose members were also involved in manufacturing.

Congregationalism is the other denomination which produced a particularly large number of Victorian industrialists. It is represented in this book by Titus Salt, Samuel Morley and William Lever. Other Congregationalists who founded firms which have continued to this day include Thomas Beecham, Thomas Holloway's great rival in the pill and patent medicine business, Sir Francis Crossley, the Halifax carpet manufacturer, and W.D. and

H.O.Wills, the Bristol cigarette makers. Alongside Jesse Boot in the Methodist gallery of fame we can put W.H.Smith, founder of the chain of retail newsagents now found on nearly every High Street and railway station, William Hartley who established the biggest jam factory in England, and Sir George Chubb who set up the lock and safe company which still bears his name. Rather fewer entrepreneurs were drawn from the ranks of the Baptists, although there is one other familiar business name from that denomination which we can add to that of Jeremiah Colman: Thomas Cook the travel agent who began his business career by organizing the transport arrangements for temperance rallies and Sunday School outings.

There is one denomination which is not represented in this book but which produced several leading industrialists in nineteenth-century Britain and that is the Unitarians. From their ranks came Samuel Courtauld whose successful weaving of silk and exploitation of the enormous Victorian demand for black crêpe for mourning wear created the firm that eventually took over Morleys, Sir Henry Tate, founder of the giant sugar producer, Tate & Lyle, and Sir John Brunner who established the chemical firm which was to become the nucleus of Imperial Chemical Industries.

These other Nonconformist industrialists share much in common with the ten figures who are the special concern of this book. Apart from their common Nonconformist faith and outlook, they were nearly all active Liberals and generous philanthropists. Many came from similarly humble backgrounds and they all displayed the same energy and vigour in seizing opportunities and building up businesses which in most cases are still flourishing.

It is, of course, true that they operated in a highly favourable environment. Although the first of the entrepreneurs featured here was born in 1800 and the last did not die until 1931 they all saw their businesses take off during the thirty-year period between 1850 and 1880 when the British economy was at its most dynamic. Those three decades saw a virtual doubling in the country's Gross National Income, a population increase of more than 25 per cent, a massive shift of people from the countryside to towns and a steady rise in real wages. Among the consequences of these trends was a booming manufacturing industry meeting unprecedented demand from both home and overseas and the creation of a mass consumer market.

The actions of successive governments considerably helped to stimulate industry and trade. The steady move towards free trade was of particular importance. Sir Robert Peel's abolition of the Corn Laws in 1846 brought down the price of wheat as a raw material and enabled firms like Huntley & Palmers to go into biscuit production on a large scale. Had Gladstone not removed the excise duty on soap and reduced the import duty on cocoa beans in his budget of 1853 it is doubtful if either Lever or Cadbury would be the household names that they are now. Gladstone's move in the same budget to abolish the high tax on newspaper advertisements (one shilling and sixpence on each insertion) and his subsequent abolition of both the stamp duty on newspapers and the excise duty on paper led to the development of the cheap mass-circulation press that was to be the main advertising medium for Thomas Holloway and Jesse Boot. Later measures, like the Sale of Food and Drugs Act of 1875 and the Trade Marks Act of the same year, greatly helped the development of Cadbury's and Colman's businesses as we shall see.

There were other factors peculiar to this period which greatly helped those with entrepreneurial instincts. The opening up of the country through the spread of railways created a unique opportunity to develop new markets and drastically reduce transport costs on both raw materials and distribution. In America, the coming of the railroad brought an even greater opportunity to Andrew Carnegie, as he saw first the profits to be made through investment in the new system and then its insatiable appetite for iron and steel. The absence of organized trade unionism in the manufacturing sector and the rising standard of living for industrial workers encouraged a generally optimistic and co-operative outlook among employees which was reinforced by the prevailing ideologies of Liberalism and Nonconformity. Strikes were few and far between, demarcation disputes and restrictive practices virtually unheard of.

The scope for philanthropy was also considerably greater then than it is now. For most of the period between 1850 and 1914 there was nothing approaching the Welfare State as we know it today. Public provision of education, health care and social services was rudimentary where it existed at all and on the whole the illiterate, the sick and the poor had to depend on charity and mutual support to alleviate their suffering. The latter part of the nineteenth century was the golden age of private philanthropy in Britain. *The Times* reported in 1885 that charitable receipts in London alone amounted to more than double the total national budget of Switzerland, while a survey a few years later found that middle-class families on average spent just over 10 per cent of their incomes on charitable donations, more than they spent on rent, clothing or servants' wages. There was a general expectation that those with wealth would give away substantial sums for philanthropic purposes and this was encouraged by low rates of direct taxation.

But even allowing for these special circumstances, it is hard to avoid the conclusion that those whose lives and achievements form the subject of this book were exceptional members of an exceptional generation. Their considerable achievements in the fields of both commercial success and social progress cannot just be explained by the particular environment in which they lived and worked. Equally important, if not more so, were their formidable energy and drive, their deep inner faith and sense of purpose and not least their enormous capacity for sheer hard work.

1
THOMAS HOLLOWAY
(1800–83)

Thomas Holloway is in many ways the odd man out among the great industrialists featured in this book. He was not a Nonconformist but a member of the Church of England and religion does not seem to have been the driving force either in his working life or in his philanthropic activities. Although there is some evidence that he was a Liberal in politics, he was not active in this sphere and took no part in civic or national affairs. He was, indeed, an exceedingly private man. He was also something of a scamp and was not above sharp commercial practice of a kind that would not have met with approval from the high-minded figures whom we shall meet in later chapters. Yet he fully deserves to be counted among the enlightened entrepreneurs of Victorian Britain.

The two institutions which he founded, Royal Holloway College and the Holloway Sanatorium, were among the largest single philanthropic enterprises undertaken by any individual in the nineteenth century. They were built, one as a university college for girls and the other as a lunatic asylum for the middle classes, out of the profits of the manufacture and sale of patent pills and ointment. By a combination of hard work and brilliant publicity, Holloway built up a worldwide business and in a little over thirty years he amassed profits of over £1 million. It took him a further ten years to dispose of this wealth in his two great philanthropic ventures. On the whole, he found it harder work spending money than making it.

The sale of patent proprietary medicines was a booming business in the nineteenth century. Qualified doctors were few and far between and their fees were beyond the range of the majority of the population, a typical consultation costing seven shillings and sixpence when average take-home pay was less than two and sixpence a week. There was also still a good deal of suspicion of the medical profession. Rural traditions of herbal remedies and old wives' cures lingered among those who moved from the countryside into the polluted and insanitary atmosphere of the new industrial towns and cities. Victorian families were easy targets for advertisements which promised prevention or cure of all manner of ailments through the simple and relatively cheap expedient of taking pills or applying ointments which could be bought over the counter. Thomas Holloway was one of the first to make his fortune by exploiting this rapidly expanding market, but he was certainly not the last. Between 1850 and 1900 the annual sales of proprietary remedies went up from £500,000 to over £4,000,000 and the number of patent medicine vendors increased from around 10,000 to over 40,000. They included the founders of two great pharmaceutical firms which are still well known today, Thomas Beecham and Jesse Boot, the subject of a later chapter in this book.

Thomas Holloway was born in 1800 in the seaside town of Devonport where his father, a former sailor, kept a public house. Soon after his birth his parents moved to Penzance in Cornwall, where they set up a grocery and bakery business, and it was there that he was apprenticed to a chemist after he left school. Following the death of his father he helped his mother behind the counter of her shop. In 1828 he left home and after a period in France he settled in London where he worked in various jobs, including that of translator. In 1836 he opened a business as a merchant and foreign commercial agent in Broad Street Buildings in the City of London.

Holloway first seems to have become involved with the sale of patent medicines when he became agent for Thomas Albinolo, an Italian manufacturer of pills and ointments who was also a vendor of leeches. In October 1837 an advertisement for Holloway's ointment appeared in three Sunday papers. It included a testimonial from a leading surgeon at St Thomas's Hospital vouching for its curative properties. Albinolo later protested that

Holloway had used his patent formula, but as he was thrown into a debtors' prison soon afterwards he was unable to press the charge.

Whether the recipe which Holloway used was his own or Albinolo's we shall never know. He made his first batches of ointment in an old saucepan of his mother's which held 6 quarts. As orders increased he changed to a long fish-kettle and then to a copper which held about 40 pounds. The ointment contained lanolin (fatty matter extracted from sheep's wool), liquid paraffin, terebinth (turpentine), yellow and white beeswax, cetaceum (whale oil), oil of theobromine (a substance similar to caffeine obtained from the seeds of the cacao tree), phenol (a derivative of benzine) and rectified oleum picis (oil of pitch). It was advertised as 'the only reliable remedy for bad legs, sores, ulcers and old wounds, for bronchitis, sore throats, coughs, colds, gout, rheumatism, glandular swellings and all skin diseases'. A selection of the earthenware pots in which the ointment was sold is on display at Egham Museum. They are decorated with a portrait of Hygeia, the Greek goddess of health, holding a child and leaning against a pillar bearing the motto 'Never Despair'.

The production of pills began two years later in 1839. Holloway made them, with the help of an old clerk, on a machine in the cellars of the Broad Street office and they were stored in one of the drawers of his desk. The ingredients changed over the years, but included aloes, known for their bitter taste and strong purgative properties, and powdered ginger, which was said to promote belching and relieve spasms of the bowel. The pills, which were sugar coated, also contained powdered jalop (obtained from the root of a Mexican climbing plant) and cambogia (a gum resin obtained from trees native in Cambodia), which were both strong purgatives, rhubarb root, cinnamon, cardamom, saffron, sodium sulphate, potassium sulphate and either hard soap or confection of roses to bind the other ingredients together.

Legend has it that Holloway began his career as a patent medicine vendor with a borrowed £5 note and that he employed his brother Henry to go round shops asking for Holloway's pills and ointments and expressing great surprise that such efficacious medicines were not in stock. Later in the day Thomas would

13

appear apparently by chance in the same shops and sell large quantities of his remedies to the well-primed shopkeepers who were now only too anxious to atone for their previous ignorance of this obviously excellent product. Whether the story is true or not, it is clear that Henry Holloway was not prepared to play second fiddle to his brother for ever. In 1850 he set up his own shop in the Strand and started selling Thomas's pills and ointments which he passed off as his own until he was restrained by a High Court injunction.

Another clever way in which Thomas Holloway built up his sales was by visiting the London Docks and offering those who were about to embark on the long journey to America a powerful laxative made of castor oil and ginger to counteract the effects of a diet of ship's biscuits. It was almost certainly on his visits to the docks that he met and courted his future wife, Jane Driver, who was the daughter of a Rotherhithe shipwright. While there, he also picked the brains of merchants and sea captains in pursuit of his dream of 'girdling the globe with depots of my remedies'.

Holloway's medicines were, indeed, destined to find their way into every corner of the world but it was to take thirty years of unremitting toil and assiduous salesmanship before they did so. These were the two foundations on which Holloway's great commercial success was based. He regularly and unstintingly applied himself for up to eighteen hours a day to the various departments of his business, taking virtually no holidays and pursuing few interests and recreations outside his work. Careful with money, he spent very little on himself but committed considerable amounts to advertising and publicity.

Holloway's early experiences with advertising could well have put him off ever using the medium again. In one week when he was first establishing his business he spent £100 on advertisements and saw only one pot of ointment sold. Some of his early publicity ventures were over-extravagant. In 1838 he spent £1,000 to have his name mentioned in London pantomimes. There is also a story that he offered a similar sum to Charles Dickens to have his pills mentioned in each chapter of his novel *Dombey and Son* when it first appeared in monthly serial form in 1847. He was for a brief period incarcerated in the debtors' prison at Whitecross Street, having found himself unable to pay his bills for newspaper advertisements. However, with the aid of a loan of £600 from his mother he was able to pay off his creditors with a bonus of 10 per cent, and he was soon back in business and advertising again.

By the early 1860s Holloway was spending more than £40,000 a year on advertising while testimonials to the efficacy of his medicines had been translated into most languages, including Chinese, Turkish, Armenian, Arabic, Sanskrit and most of the Indian vernaculars. His name was to be found on children's atlases and drawing books and had even appeared inscribed on banners draped over the great pyramid in Egypt and beside the Niagara Falls. By the end of his life his advertising budget stood at over £1,000 a week.

Press advertisements were the main type of publicity that Holloway used. They took the form of statements from well-known medical figures testifying to the therapeutic properties of his ointments and pills. These were supplemented by publications giving more detailed information, like *Holloway's Abridged Medical Guide for the use of missionaries and others who kindly interest themselves in recommending the use of its remedies*. Written by Holloway himself, who adopted the title of Professor for the purposes of such scientific treatises, this authoritatively proclaimed: 'All diseases have one primary cause, viz. a want of purity in the blood and fluids, and consequently can alone be cured by their purification. The specific force of the balsamic remedy here introduced exerts itself so that it searches out and removes complaints of every character.' The guide went on to recommend the pills and ointment for diseases of the liver, stomach and bowels, indigestion and nervous disorder, sunstroke, rheumatism, ague, yellow fever, scurvy, scorbutic affections, ringworms and scaldheads, other worms, diseases of the throat and chest, influenza, bronchitis, piles, sores and ulcers, mosquito bites, dropsy and female complaints. On this last subject, the guide informed women 'in difficult stages of life' that 'if these purifying pills be kept at hand and used with discretion, they will ward off all dangers to which the sex at such ages is liable'.

15

Another important advertising medium was Holloway's *Almanac and Family Friend* which appeared annually. As well as containing much useful general information, like the results of the Oxford and Cambridge boat race over the past thirty years, this graphically described a different disease every month with the invariable advice that it could be relieved by copious quantities of the pills or ointment. Readers were advised that the ointment should be 'well rubbed over the spleen, liver and kidneys, night and morning, in considerable quantities' while the pills should be taken 'in doses sufficient to cause the bowels to act freely (but gently) once a day'. The recommended dose varied from two a day to seven both morning and evening.

There is a striking contrast between the bold and extravagant claims that Holloway was happy to make in his advertisements and the simplicity and even drudgery of his own lifestyle. In 1839, following his release from the debtors' prison, he moved to a small building in the Strand. For nearly thirty years this was to be home, office, factory, warehouse and shop. Thomas and Jane, who married in 1840, were up at four most mornings to start mixing the medicines and packing the day's orders, and were often still toiling over the accounts until ten at night. In 1867 the building was demolished to make way for the new Law Courts and the Holloways moved to larger premises in Oxford Street. Despite the fact that their personal wealth now stood at over £250,000 they continued to live above the shop and occupied a suite of rooms on the top floor of the five-storey building. Below them were the counting house, manufacturing department and packaging rooms where, in the words of the *Pall Mall Gazette*, young women filled boxes 'from small hillocks of pills each containing a sufficient dose for a whole city'.

Obtaining satisfactory supplies of the circular wooden boxes into which the pills were packed proved to be one of the most troublesome areas of the whole business. They came in four sizes, ranging from $1\frac{1}{2}$ to $3\frac{1}{2}$ inches in diameter. Holloway was constantly complaining that those supplied to him were not of the right dimensions nor of uniform size, that the wood was damp, and that the boxes were too deep with the result that customers complained

16

that they got short measure. He found British suppliers particularly unsatisfactory and increasingly turned to Continental firms for his boxes. The pots for his ointment came from Staffordshire and seem to have presented fewer problems.

Another major problem that Holloway faced was the counterfeiting of his medicines abroad. He had opened an agency in the United States in the 1850s and by the late 1860s his pills and ointments were well known and in considerable demand in many parts of the world. Customers included the King of Siam, the Maharajah of Bulrampore and His Highness Meerally Moorad Kahn. This success led to the appearance of many pirate versions of Holloway's medicines. In 1870 he discovered that pills were being made in Hamburg and sold to South America under his name. He warned M.T.Bass, the Burton-on-Trent brewer, that the same thing was happening to his beer. The counterfeiting was particularly bad in the United States where there was a large demand for Holloway's ointment. In an effort to frustrate it, he had the American labels of his products frequently changed.

One of the most important jobs of the overseas agents whom Holloway employed was to bring legal actions against counterfeiters. A contract with a new Italian agent, Pelayo Montoya, in 1871 mentions pirate manufacturers in Florence. It is also interesting in showing the hard bargain that Holloway struck with his agents. Montoya was to be on a short-term contract, send in twice-weekly reports on sales and agree not to work for any other firm. For this he was to be paid £4 a week, plus travelling expenses, always providing that he paid due regard to the need for economy, 'travelling upon all occasions by 2nd class conveyance and going to such hotels only as are most in repute with commercial travellers'.

Holloway seems to have adopted a generally benevolent and enlightened attitude towards his employees, who numbered around a hundred in the Oxford Street premises. He employed a doctor to look after their health and insisted on paying each of his staff personally every day. After his experiences in the debtors' prison he resolved that he would never again be in debt to anyone, and this meant not even owing wages for a period of a week. So everyone was paid by the day and he always kept a bag of sovereigns handy so that debts to suppliers and tradesmen could be discharged equally promptly. Like many Victorian employers he believed in rewarding his workers on the occasion of anniversaries in the life of the firm and in using such celebrations as the opportunity for moral exhortation. In 1877, for example, he celebrated the fortieth anniversary of the business by presenting a gold sovereign to each of his twenty-three clerks, five shillings to each of the twelve porters and two shillings and sixpence to each of the thirty-six girls in the packing department. Before receiving these gifts, the assembled staff were treated to an account of their boss's rise from his humble origins and reminded 'what small beginnings may lead to, by ability, perseverance and industry'.

By the early 1870s Thomas Holloway, now in his seventies and one of the richest men in Britain, with annual profits of around £50,000, might well have been expected to retire. It is true that he ceased his daily involvement in the business, which he handed over to his brother-in-law, Henry Driver, and exchanged his flat above the office for a country house near Sunninghill on the Middlesex–Surrey border. But retirement from business did not for him mean a life of indolence and leisure. For the last ten years of his life he devoted himself as single-mindedly and assiduously to the task of giving away his wealth as he had in the past three decades to the business of accumulating it.

Holloway had no children to whom to pass on his wealth and this fact may well have influenced him in his decision to engage in large-scale philanthropy. While building up his business he does not appear to have shown any interest in charitable activity. Indeed, he deplored conventional charity and 'good works', believing that they pauperized their recipients. But in the 1860s he began looking around for some socially useful projects to which he could devote his considerable accumulation of capital. He was keen not to scatter his bounty over a wide variety of causes but rather to concentrate his giving and find one or two specific ventures to support. He was also keen that his philanthropy should take the form of bricks and mortar and that his wealth should endow a new institution.

For advice on which particular project he should take up Holloway turned to one of the great philanthropic figures of the Victorian age, the 7th Earl of Shaftesbury, famous as the champion of the cause of factory children. In 1861 Shaftesbury had spoken at a public meeting in London about the plight of those in the middle and professional classes who fell victim to mental illness. Unable to pay the fees charged by the first-class establishments which catered for the aristocracy, they were often unable to gain places in the overcrowded pauper asylums. Holloway was in the audience and was much moved by the earl's call for the establishment of a mental hospital specifically for the middle classes. In 1864 he went to see Shaftesbury and told him of his plan to commit £250,000 to a single charitable purpose. As a result of this meeting Holloway decided to found a sanatorium.

Detailed planning for the project began in 1871. Holloway interested himself in every detail and visited lunatic asylums up and down the country, cross-examining doctors about the treatment of the mentally ill. He even inquired whether tea or coffee would be the more suitable beverage for nervous and insane patients. He was determined that his should be a model institution breaking new ground in the treatment of the mentally ill. It was to be a curative establishment rather than a mere asylum. 'The medical staff', he wrote, 'will do everything that is possible to cure their patients and return them to their friends, whereas in the ordinary way if it is a pay patient it is to the interest of the Proprietor to keep them, and if at a Pauper Lunatic Asylum the patient is herded with the rest and lost sight of'.

Holloway was determined that his sanatorium should have 500 rooms and be set in 20 acres of ground. He wanted it to be about fifteen miles from London and plainly visible from a railway line. It is not quite clear whether he made this last stipulation in order that the results of his benevolence should be on public view or as a deliberate gesture against the traditional isolation of mental institutions. The site that he eventually chose, on St Ann's Heath near Virginia Water in north-west Surrey, was, in fact, visible from two railway lines and had the additional advantage that part of the land was already his.

19

He had made up his mind that the sanatorium should be built in brick, a material which was easily available in the neighbourhood, and in what he called 'the grand old Flemish style'. A competition was held to find a design and the winner was W. H. Crossland, the architect of Rochdale Town Hall and of the model industrial community of Akroydon, near Halifax. He produced plans for a building which was closely modelled on the cloth hall in the Belgian town of Ypres and which was in the words of the distinguished architectural historian, Sir Nikolaus Pevsner, 'a sort of Franco-Flemish brick-and-stone and Gothic'.

A prospectus for the sanatorium was issued in 1872. It made clear that the establishment was 'not intended for pauper patients but for persons of the reduced middle class'. The inmates were to be provided with a 'noble hall' for dining, a billiard room, and a Turkish bath, and there was to be ample accommodation for servants. The prospectus also promised that the sexes would be segregated with male patients' rooms on one side of the central clock tower and females' rooms on the other.

The first brick of the new building was laid by Mrs Holloway in 1873, the occasion being marked by a gift of £1 to every workman. Thomas Holloway supervised every aspect of construction and engaged in vigorous negotiations with suppliers to get the cheapest possible terms. He himself purchased the bricks and then resold them to the contractor. He personally bought everything else that was required, even down to the wheelbarrows. As in his business, every workman on the site was paid by the day.

With the sanatorium now under way, Holloway turned his mind to another great philanthropic venture. It seems to have been from his wife Jane that he got the idea of founding a university college for women. He had originally intended to establish a hospital for incurables, but Jane beseeched him to spend part of his fortune on a benefaction for women 'because they are the greatest sufferers'. The principle of higher education for women was only just beginning to take root in Britain. The first women's college had been founded by Miss Anne Clough in 1869. Originally sited at Hitchin, Hertfordshire, it moved to the village of Girton, near Cambridge, in 1873. It was in that year that Jane Holloway died and Thomas resolved to build a college as a memorial to her. As with the sanatorium, he wanted to find an elevated site visible from some distance, and in 1874 he bought a 93-acre plot on Egham Hill, also in north-west Surrey. Here, he announced, was to be built 'Holloway College, to afford the best education suitable for women of the middle and upper middle classes'.

Holloway decided to avoid the trouble of another architects' competition and commissioned Crossland to design the new building. This time the style chosen was French Renaissance and it was resolved to make the college an almost exact replica of the château of Chambord on the Loire. Crossland was dispatched to France with an assistant to measure the château 'from bottom to top' and Holloway later joined him there to check the work and study other châteaux. Altogether it took Crossland two years to draw up plans for the college, which was to be built around two massive quadrangles with rooms for 300 students and 100 servants in addition to lecture rooms, chapel, dining room, library and a generous supply of common rooms (one for every six students) for 'tea and toast parties'. The whole building was to be faced in red brick, with ornate towers. Pevsner describes the finished product as 'the most ebullient Victorian building in the Home Counties ... a stupendous paraphrase of the French 16th Century Renaissance, combining a brilliant decorative sense with utter self-confidence'.

Work on the college began in 1879. As with the sanatorium, Holloway carefully scrutinized every item of expenditure. Although he only visited the building site four times, he drove past it in his carriage every day and received daily reports from his wife's brother-in-law, George Martin, who supervised operations on site. Between 1881 and 1883 he spent £85,000 on buying seventy-seven paintings by leading contemporary artists like Landseer, Frith and Millais to hang in the students' recreation hall. They still hang there today, although one, Landseer's *Man Proposes, God Disposes*, is regularly covered with a Union Jack as it is considered unlucky for any examination candidate to sit beneath it.

Despite the fact that he was now in his eighties Holloway also busied himself with planning the academic and administrative arrangements for the college. He was assisted by a powerful team of advisers which included Samuel Morley and Emily Davies, the foundress of Girton College, Cambridge. Modern feminists might cavil at his motives for wanting to improve the education of women as expressed in his statement 'How much do we not owe to our dear mother's early training, and as she has been trained she will in most cases instil the same training into the minds of her children to benefit this commercial country'. The foundation deeds which he drew up in 1883, however, show a remarkably enlightened approach. They were strongly influenced by the principles which the American philanthropist, Matthew Vassar, had laid down when founding his college for women in New York in 1861. Holloway wanted something more than just 'a mere training college for teachers and governesses'. He stated his conviction that 'the education of women should not be exclusively regulated by the traditions and methods of former ages, but that it should be founded on those studies and sciences which the experience of modern times has shown to be the most valuable and best adapted to meet the intellectual and social requirements of the students'. Proficiency in classics was not to be regarded as the highest intellectual attainment and the examination for admission was to test English, foreign languages, mathematics and physical science.

Rather surprisingly, Holloway provided no science laboratories in the college and they had to be fitted in later in the basements. He did provide a chapel but stipulated that no permanent chaplain should be appointed 'and no arrangement made which would identify the college in any way with any particular sect or denomination'. He was also emphatic that no student or teacher should be required to submit to any test of religious opinion as a condition of admission or appointment. This did not mean that he wished the college to be based on secularist principles. He made a point of stating in the foundation deeds that he himself had throughout his life 'witnessed the hand of God in all things' and of making clear that he wished the teaching in the college to be 'such as to impress most forcibly on the minds of the students their individual responsibility and their duty to God'. The overall atmosphere was to be 'that of an orderly Christian household' and with this in mind he laid down that the lady principal should every morning during term conduct a simple service with a psalm or hymn, a reading from Scripture and prayers.

The foundation deeds laid down that the principal must be more than forty at the time of her appointment and that she should be required to resign on reaching the age of sixty-five. She would also have to resign if she got married and the same rule applied to all of the resident tutors, who were required to be either spinsters or widows without issue. No male teacher was to reside in the college at any time. One wonders if W.S.Gilbert had Royal Holloway College in mind when he created the women's university of Castle Adamant for his comic opera *Princess Ida*, which was first performed in January 1884. Certainly the following piece of dialogue could well have been inspired by a perusal of the foundation deeds:

Florian: Are there no males whatever in those walls?
Gama: None, gentlemen, excepting letter-mails –
   And they are driven (as males often are
   In other large communities) by women.
   Why, bless my heart, she's so particular
   She'll scarcely suffer Dr. Watts's hymns –
   And all the animals she owns are 'hers'!
   The ladies rise at cockcrow every morn –
Cyril: Ah, then they have male poultry?
Gama: Not at all,
   The crowing's done by an accomplished hen!

In choosing the college governing body Holloway showed his dislike for the professional upper middle classes and his preference for self-made men like himself. He wanted to exclude clergymen, doctors and lawyers from ever being governors but was dissuaded from taking such a rigid line. His first team of governors included two Liberal MPs, Samuel Morley and David Chadwick. This is one of the few indications we have of Holloway's Liberal sympathies. Another is the fact that he had a meeting with William Ewart Gladstone in 1873. The prime minister recorded 'Had a long conversation with Mr Holloway (of the pills) on his philanthropic plans which are very interesting'. There is some suggestion that Gladstone may have offered Holloway a baronetcy after this meeting, but if so, the honour was declined.

Sadly, Thomas Holloway did not live to see either his college or his sanatorium completed and opened. He died in December 1883 and was interred in a massive red granite tomb in the churchyard of St Michael's, Sunninghill. The sanatorium was opened in June 1885 by the Prince and Princess of Wales on their way to attend the Ascot races. The college was opened by Queen Victoria in June 1886. The front quadrangle contains an imposing statue of the queen with her arm resting on the throne. In the middle of the back quadrangle there is a statue of Thomas and Jane Holloway, she sitting with the plans of the college on her lap while he stands with one arm resting on her shoulder and the other pointing into the distance. Around the base of the statue are four maidens, two with books, one with a pestle and mortar and one gazing out at the world. Holloway's motto 'Nil Desperandum' is inscribed on the base and a plaque on the back records:

THOMAS HOLLOWAY. BORN 1800. DIED 1883.
HE FOUNDED AND ENDOWED THIS COLLEGE IN MEMORY OF HIS
WIFE JANE, BORN 1814. DIED 1875.
HE ALSO FOUNDED THE HOLLOWAY SANATORIUM,
BOTH INSTITUTIONS BEING A FREE GIFT TO THE NATION.

Altogether Thomas Holloway spent about £800,000 on his college and £300,000 on his sanatorium. His decision to devote his wealth to establishing these two institutions does not seem to have been taken out of guilt or out of any strong religious conviction or political philosophy. They were not the culmination of a lifetime's interest in social problems or education. Rather, Holloway simply seems to have come to the view at the end of his life that he wished to use his accumulated wealth for some socially useful purpose, and to have taken advice from others on what that purpose should be. In the words of *The Times*, 'His munificence is as innocently neutral as are said to be his own drugs'.

There is something enigmatic about Holloway's character. The buildings which he created were, like the advertisements for his medicines, extravagant and even fanciful. They reveal a touch of the showman and the egotist. Yet in his philanthropy as in his business life Holloway was meticulously careful, studiously diligent and strangely self-effacing. His private life was modest and simple. He had few friends outside his immediate family and had no taste for social engagements or parties. He steered well clear of the fashionable high society world into which his wealth could easily have admitted him. His tastes were modest – he drank nothing stronger than claret and water and apparently had no pastimes beyond riding in his carriage. His one indulgence was buying paintings, both the fine collection of contemporary British works which he amassed for the college and an important group of Old Masters which he bought for his home at Sunninghill.

After his death the manufacture and sale of Holloway's medicines were taken over by his wife's brother, Henry Driver, and her brother-in-law, George Martin, both of whom added Holloway to their surnames in accordance with a promise they had made to Thomas. Their two families continued the business until 1929 when it was taken over by J. Stanley Holmes. The following year it was acquired by Beechams who marketed Holloway's pills and ointment until 1950. Ironically, the founder of Beechams had been one of Thomas Holloway's greatest rivals, who had risen from similarly humble origins. Thomas Beecham (1820–1907) started making pills by hand while working as a shepherd boy in Oxfordshire, went north to Wigan in Lancashire, where he opened a shop selling patent medicines in 1847, and established a factory at nearby St Helen's in the 1860s. Like Holloway, he built up his business largely on the basis of advertising, using to great effect as a slogan a chance remark of one of his customers that his pills were worth a guinea a box.

Holloway's pills and ointment may have gone the way of other now forgotten Victorian patent remedies, like Dr Collis Brown's compound, Elliman's Universal Embrocation, Widow Welch's pills and the Carbolic Smoke Ball, but the two ornate piles which he constructed remain as monuments to the profitability of this once flourishing trade. They have been justly described by Sir Nikolaus Pevsner as 'the summit of High Victorian design'. Silhouetted like fairy castles against the sky, they are clearly visible from the M25 motorway south-west of London and provide a dramatic diversion from the vista of concrete flyovers and underpasses in the vicinity of the turn-off to Heathrow Airport. Holloway Sanatorium is no longer a mental hospital – it was closed down by Surrey Health Authority in 1981, since when its Gothic façade has been much used by film companies making horror movies, and is now being converted into offices. Holloway College became part of London University in 1900 and in 1985 it merged with Bedford College to form Royal Holloway and Bedford New College. Thomas Holloway's country house has meanwhile passed to the purveyors of what has perhaps been the twentieth century's most popular patent drug – pop music. It was for many years owned by John Lennon and is now the home of another ex-Beatle, Ringo Starr.

2
SIR TITUS SALT
(1803–76)

Several men have given their names to individual buildings and streets in Britain, but very few to entire communities. The model village of Saltaire was founded by Sir Titus Salt in the 1850s, on the banks of the River Aire near Bradford, to house the workers employed in what was then the largest textile mill in the world. Still very much a living community today, it is a remarkable memorial to one of the most energetic and enlightened figures in British industrial history.

Sir Titus Salt was in many ways the archetypal Victorian industrialist. He rose from comparatively humble origins by dint of hard work and commercial acumen to become one of the richest and most powerful of the West Riding textile barons, directly employing more than 3,500 hands. An ardent Congregationalist, a strict teetotaller and a campaigner for temperance reform, he embodied the stern but enlightened values of the Nonconformist Conscience. He was involved in many of the great radical and reforming movements of his day and took a prominent part in Liberal politics. As an employer he was a true paternalist, taking his workers out of the polluted environment of Bradford, providing them with good housing and amenities and expecting them in return to be sober, God fearing and hard working.

Titus Salt was born in 1803 in the West Yorkshire village of Morley, the eldest of seven children. His grandfather had been a tinsmith in Sheffield and his father, Daniel, was a white-cloth merchant and dry salter dealing in chemical products. Daniel later became a farmer, moving the family to a small village near Wakefield. Titus attended a school in the town which had been set up to provide 'a plain commercial education', travelling in from the country on a donkey with his sister riding pillion behind him.

As a boy he wanted to become a doctor. He was put off this course, however, when at the age of seventeen he cut himself badly while chopping some wood. He fainted at the sight of so much blood and when he came round it was to hear his father saying 'Titus, my lad, thou wilt never be a doctor'. Instead, he was apprenticed to a woolstapler in Wakefield to learn the rudiments of the woollen textile trade in which West Yorkshire was already beginning to lead the world.

In 1822 Daniel Salt gave up farming and moved to the rapidly expanding town of Bradford to set up in business as a woolstapler. Titus was apprenticed to an older-established Bradford firm to master the skills of wool stapling. He learned how to buy good fleeces at auction, how to sort out the wool according to the length, fineness and softness of its fibre, and how to wash and comb it in preparation for spinning into yarn. Characteristically, he remained an apprentice for two years until he had thoroughly mastered each of these processes and it was not until he was twenty-one that he joined his father's firm of Daniel Salt & Son as wool buyer. His main job was to attend sheep clippings in the Yorkshire dales, Norfolk and Lincolnshire and auctions of imported fleeces at the London and Liverpool docks. It was on one of his trips to Lincolnshire that he met and fell in love with a farmer's daughter, Caroline Whitlam, who in 1829 became his bride.

Despite his constant travelling, Titus Salt rapidly established himself as a lively and energetic force in the religious and civic life of Bradford. He was actively involved in the affairs of the Horton Lane Congregational Chapel where he held the offices of librarian, teacher and superintendent of the Sunday School. He was also sworn in as a special constable and helped to quell violent demonstrations on the part of striking mill workers.

On his buying trips around the country Salt was constantly on the lookout for new materials. He bought a large quantity of Donskoi wool from south-east Russia which had been rejected by other manufacturers. Unable to find anyone prepared to spin it, he tried himself and found that it made a very good worsted yarn. This experiment led to the opening of a spinning mill in Bradford. In 1833 Daniel Salt retired and Titus took over the business, concentrating as much on spinning and weaving as on preparing the wool. He continued his search for new materials, at one stage even trying to see if he could spin yarn from the fibres of the seaweed which grew in copious quantities on the beach at Scarborough.

One day in 1834, while on a buying visit to Liverpool docks, he noticed a pile of 300 or so dirty-looking bales lying in the corner of a warehouse. They turned out to be fleeces of the alpaca, an animal closely related to the llama and native to Peru. Out of interest Salt pulled out a handful of the evil-smelling wool and examined it. He was impressed by the straightness and length of the fibres. Several weeks later he returned to the warehouse where the fleeces were still lying forlorn and unwanted. This time Salt took a sample back to Bradford in his handkerchief and experimented with spinning it. He found that it produced a high-quality glossy yarn. To the astonishment and delight of the brokers, who had long given up all hope of selling them, he offered to buy the alpaca fleeces at eight-pence a pound.

Salt's chance discovery on the quayside started a new industry which was to make Bradford and the surrounding district one of the most prosperous regions of Britain over the next half-century. It took considerable time and patience to spin and weave the alpaca into cloth but once the necessary machinery and techniques had been perfected the result was a material which had the gloss and rustling 'frou-frou' effect of silk but at much less cost and with greater durability. In 1837 Salt introduced Alpaca Orleans, a fabric made of cotton and alpaca, which became a favourite dress material with Victorian ladies for the next fifty years. With its stiffness and its lustrous sheen, achieved by stretching the cotton warp and bringing the alpaca weft to the surface, it was particularly suitable for crinolines and was also in heavy demand for mourning wear. The success of the fabric was assured when Queen Victoria sent Salt the fleeces of the two alpacas she kept in Windsor Park to be made up into cloth.

By 1839 the price of alpaca wool had risen to thirty pence a pound and two million pounds of it was being imported every year, much of it destined for Salt's mills. He was also making much use of mohair, another long-staple combing wool, which came from the fleece of the angora goat found in Turkey and which also produced a fine lustrous cloth when combined with cotton. It was through his exploitation of the properties of these two unusual wools that Salt was to establish his position as king of the burgeoning West Yorkshire worsted industry and accumulate a personal fortune.

In 1844 he moved his wife and eleven children out of the increasingly polluted and noisy environment of Bradford to a large house at Lightcliffe about ten miles outside the city. But, although he was now rich and secure enough to do so, he did not take up the lifestyle of a country gentleman. He was at his mill by six o'clock every morning, before the machines started turning and often before the first worker arrived. It was later said of him that he made £1,000 a day before his rivals were out of bed. He was a fanatic for punctuality, both in his mills where lateness was punished and at home where he demanded prompt attendance at meals and family prayers. He had iron self-discipline and expected the same from others, but he was also remarkably generous. On the way to work he often stopped his carriage to give £5 to an employee whom he knew to have been ill or in difficulties.

Salt's generosity showed itself in the year that he spent as mayor of Bradford. He took on the office in November 1848 at a time of acute distress and high unemployment throughout Britain, and particularly in Bradford where the quality textile market had been depressed as a result of revolutions on the Continent. The town was also suffering a cholera outbreak which claimed more than 400 lives. As mayor, Salt plunged himself into activity to relieve the town's problems, inaugurating a proper system of drainage and sanitation, opening soup kitchens and even devising a scheme for emigration to the New World. He also made a more personal contribution to alleviating the misery of his fellow citizens. Despite the fact that sales from his own mills had fallen by £10,000 a month because of the slump in trade, he took on 100 unemployed woolcombers and laid by their work against better times returning.

During his mayoralty Salt took a particular interest in the moral condition of the populace of Bradford. He was appalled by the misery caused to individuals and families by excessive drinking and was determined to encourage the development of alternative places of recreation and entertainment to the ubiquitous public house. He was instrumental in having St George's Hall built in the centre of the town and was also actively involved in the planning and building of music halls and mechanics' institutes where people could enjoy and improve themselves free from the temptations of alcohol. He was one of the first employers in the area to grant a half holiday on Saturdays, believing that it might end the rush from the factory gates into the pub which took place every Saturday evening and often resulted in workers drinking away much of their weekly wages before they returned to their wives and families.

In his concern with punctuality, sobriety and self-improvement Salt was very much a man of his time. But in one important respect he was very much ahead of it. He realized the importance of environmental factors in determining people's behaviour. He did not believe that anything excused the drunkenness, the violence and the indolence of many of the poorer classes in Bradford but he realized that these vices were encouraged by the terrible conditions in which many people lived and that they would not be eradicated unless housing, sanitation and working conditions in the town were radically improved.

Mid-nineteenth-century Bradford was the fastest growing town in the Western world. Its population increased from 43,527 in 1831 to 103,778 in 1851 as people poured in from the countryside to work in the rapidly expanding woollen textile industry. There was no time to build proper houses or to lay down proper drains to cope with this vast expansion. Bradford became the dirtiest and most insanitary place in the country with a higher proportion of malformed, undernourished and crippled children than anywhere else in England and an average life expectancy at birth of just eighteen years. Conditions were worst for the woolcombers, traditionally the lowest paid workers in the textile industry. It was not uncommon for twenty of them to live together in a cellar just 4 yards square, sleeping in rotas with four or more to a bed. Hardly surprisingly, 70 per cent of woolcombers' children died before they reached the age of fifteen.

Salt was determined to clean up this appallingly unhealthy environment. He started by trying to tackle the atmospheric pollution. Bradford had more than 200 mill chimneys emitting sulphurous fumes. Salt himself fitted special smoke burners to the chimney stacks on his own mills to reduce pollution. As mayor he tried hard to get the council to pass a by-law making such devices compulsory in all factories and mills throughout the town, but his fellow industrialists objected that this would put up their costs. Next, he sought to provide open spaces in the town where people could get away from the crowded streets and breathe some relatively fresh air. Once again he gave a personal lead by giving to the town in 1850 a 61-acre park which he named after Sir Robert Peel whose repeal of the Corn Laws four years earlier had boosted the principles of free trade which Salt, like all Victorian industrialists, held so dear. Other similar schemes followed, but by now Salt had something altogether bigger and more fundamental in mind as a solution, at least for his own workers, to problems caused by the dirt and squalor of Bradford. He was turning his mind to the creation of a model industrial community in the countryside.

Like Thomas Holloway, Titus Salt took up what was to be the great philanthropic project of his life at a time when he might have been expected to be contemplating retirement or at least an easing up in his activities. His involvement in the planning of Saltaire began when he was approaching fifty and continued until his death at the age of seventy-three. He himself later admitted that he had been briefly tempted to invest his wealth in landed property and enjoy the last twenty years of his life free from the stresses of business, but he had rejected this option for two reasons: 'In the first place, I thought that by the concentration of my works in one locality I might provide occupation for my sons. Moreover, as a landed proprietor I felt I should be out of my element. . . . Outside of my business I am nothing – in it, I have considerable influence. By the opening of Saltaire, I also hope to do good to my fellow men.'

As his remarks suggest, Salt's motives for wanting to move to what would nowadays be called a green-field site were a mixture of sound business sense and philanthropy. By 1850 he had five mills in Bradford employing more than 2,000 people. A single factory would make considerable economic sense and would enable him to take advantage of new machinery which performed the wool combing that had traditionally been done by outworkers scattered around the town. He also badly needed a better water supply than was available in Bradford. On top of this there were the undoubted benefits that his workers would gain from being moved out of the overcrowded city slums.

The site which he chose was three miles north-west of Bradford on the south bank of the River Aire. It had the advantage of superb communications, being adjacent to the Leeds–Liverpool canal, the Midland Railway line and the turnpike road from Leeds to Keighley. It was also close to the moors and to some spectacular wild scenery. In 1850, Salt commissioned two local architects to design a model industrial community.

The mill was the first building to be erected at Saltaire. It was also the world's first totally integrated woollen textile factory in which all the processes from sorting the raw, greasy fleeces to dispatching the dyed and finished cloth were brought together under one roof. Built in an Italianate style, it was supposedly modelled on Osborne House, Queen Victoria's residence on the Isle of Wight. It stood six storeys high, covered an area of $6\frac{3}{4}$ acres and was equal in length to St Paul's Cathedral. Salt was determined that his mill should be the biggest and best in Europe. The spinning hall on the top floor was, at 550 by 72 feet, easily the largest single room in the Western world. Adjoining the main building was a glass-covered weaving shed where 1,200 power looms turned out more than 18 miles of cloth a day. Salt had originally contemplated buying part of the Crystal Palace, used for the 1851 Great Exhibition, for a weaving shed but he found that it was not substantial enough to withstand the vibrations of the 3,000-horsepower engines used to drive the machinery.

Salt's mill was unprecedented not just in its size but also in its design. Large plate-glass windows and flues made the whole building light and airy. Noise was minimized by placing much of the shafting which drove the machinery under the floor, and special conduits on the roofs supplied rainwater to a 500,000-gallon reservoir. The 250-foot-high mill chimney was designed to look like the campanile of an Italian church and was fitted with a special smoke-burning device to cut down the pollution from the 50 tons of coal which were burned every day in the ten boilers.

The opening of the mill on 20 September 1853 – Salt's fiftieth birthday – was attended by 3,500 people who ate their way through 2 tons of meat, half a ton of potatoes, 320 plum puddings, 100 jellies and a mound of fruit and biscuits. The *Illustrated London News* commented that it was 'perhaps the largest dinner party ever sat down under one roof at one time'. Initially nearly all the 3,500 people who worked in the mill, or the 'Palace of Industry' as it came to be known, travelled in from Bradford every day by train, but Salt told the assembled guests at the opening that it was just the first stage in a massive building programme which would result in the creation of an entire new village. 'I will do all I can', he said, 'to avoid evils so great resulting from polluted air and water and hope to draw around me a well fed, contented and happy band of operatives. I have given instructions to my architects that nothing is to be spared to render the dwellings a pattern to the country.'

Sir Titus Salt was not the first employer to establish a model community for his workforce. In the 1800s Robert Owen, the utopian socialist, had built houses, a music hall and a ballroom for the employees of his cotton mills near Lanark in south-west Scotland. In 1846 John Grubb Richardson, a Quaker flax spinner, built the industrial village of Bessbrook, near Newry in Northern Ireland. Three years later Edward Akroyd, like Salt a West Yorkshire worsted manufacturer, began a scheme of model dwellings at Copley, near Halifax. Later he was to establish a more ambitious community called Akroydon. In the same year that Salt's mill opened William Wilson began a garden village at Bromborough Pool on the Wirral Peninsula for the employees of Price's Patent Candle Company who were moved out of London for much the same reasons that Salt's workers were transferred from Bradford. There was a general awakening of interest in working-class housing in the mid-nineteenth century stimulated partly by Lord Shaftesbury's Society for Improving the Condition of the Labouring Classes and partly by Prince Albert's model cottages which were exhibited in the 1851 Great Exhibition. Salt was undoubtedly influenced by these earlier ventures but his model village stands out both in its scale and its scope.

The dwellings in Saltaire were built over a twenty-year period. In all about 850 houses were put up, accommodating 4,500 people. The twenty-two streets were laid out according to a strict geometric plan and covered a total area of 49 acres. The main thoroughfare, which ran down to the mill, was named Victoria Road after the queen and there was also an Albert Terrace to commemorate her husband. Salt named the other principal streets after his wife and children and the architects who designed the village. The houses varied in size and grandeur according to the status of their occupants. Managers got semi-detached houses while ordinary workmen got cottages with a living room, scullery and three bedrooms. All the dwellings were well built, with gas and water laid on and back yards with privy, coalstore and ashpit – a considerable improvement on the cramped and squalid conditions of the back-to-back terraces of Bradford.

By 1856 the first houses in Saltaire were occupied and the village was beginning to take shape. The third anniversary of the opening of the mill was celebrated with a party in the grounds of Salt's house at Lightcliffe, where he kept a herd of llamas, alpacas and angora goats. More than 3,000 people came by train from Bradford and processed up to the house, led by a drum and fife band. They were rewarded for their climb by a large feast and in the evening the party transferred to St George's Hall in Bradford where Salt was presented with a marble bust by his workforce. It now stands in the entrance to the Congregational church in Saltaire. The workman who seconded the vote of thanks spoke with feeling and commendable brevity: 'Ah've wrout for sixteen yeear for Mr Salt, an 'ah can saya 'at ah am weel pleeased an' weel satisfied wi'im, an'ah second 't moation wi'all my hart, an' sit ma doan.'

Titus Salt was very clear about both what he wanted and what he did not want in his model village. He was emphatic that there was to be no public house, no pawn shop and no police station. A notice at the entrance to the village warned 'Abandon beer all ye who enter here'. Significantly, the first public building to be erected was a magnificent Congregational church in Italianate style with seating for 600. It was sited directly opposite the main entrance to the mill. Salt did not insist that his workers went to church, though it was said that they stood more chance of getting one of the better houses in Saltaire if they did so, and he certainly did not insist that, like him, they went to the Congregational church. He provided land for a Methodist chapel and was on good terms with the local Anglican church. Like all Congregationalists, he was a firm believer in religious tolerance and pluralism but for him a place of worship was a central feature of any community, second only to the workplace.

He took care to provide for the physical as well as the spiritual cleanliness of his workers. The next public building to be erected after the church was an impressive complex of public baths and wash-houses equipped with the latest in washing machines, wringers, drying frames and hot-air closets. Then came forty-five almshouses provided rent-free and with a pension of ten shillings a week to retired people 'of good moral character', schools, a hospital, a library and finally in 1870 a club and institute, the purpose of which was clearly set out in a circular sent to all the inhabitants of the village:

It is intended to supply the advantages of a public house without its evils; it will be a place to which you can resort for conversation, business, recreation and refreshment, as well as for education – elementary, technical and scientific. In the belief that 'It is gude to be merrie and wise' provision is made for innocent and intelligent recreation.

Salt was unstinting in his efforts to provide his workers with the means for innocent recreation. In 1871 he gave them a large park, laid out with cricket pitches and giving access to the beauty spot of Shipley Glen and the moors beyond. He even had the course of the River Aire altered to improve the view and allow boating and he provided a handsome boathouse. Numerous societies were started up in the village under his patronage, the most popular being the Horticultural, Pig, Dog, Poultry and Pigeon Society. He also laid on works outings with an improving flavour – in 1857, for example, he took the mill workers to the Art Treasures Exhibition in Manchester.

Life in Saltaire had a disciplined, wholesome quality. Work in the mill started at 6 a.m. and finished at 6 p.m. with an interval from 8.00 to 8.30 a.m. for breakfast and 12.30 to 1.30 p.m. for dinner. Six times a day the streets were filled with the workers hurrying to or from their homes, their clogs clattering on the cobbles. Public drunkenness and violence were virtually unknown even after an off-licence was allowed in the village in 1867. Salt banned smoking, gambling and swearing in the park and frowned on villagers hanging out washing in the streets. There may have been a slight sense among his employees that Big Brother was watching them all the time. The house occupied by the mill's security officer stood on a street corner and had a glass-windowed tower on top of the roof so, it was said, that he could observe the activities of the villagers. But in general Saltaire seems to have been a particularly happy and energetic community. When the younger Charles Dickens went there in 1857 he reported that 'all looked prosperous and happy' and another journalist who visited in 1871 noted 'a better looking body of factory "hands" I have not seen'.

For some reason Saltaire came to be known as Treacle City. According to one local theory this was because the inhabitants sat around at home eating treacle sandwiches instead of going out to public houses. Others suggest that the villagers were too poor to afford anything else. In fact, Salt paid good wages by the standards of the day and although his insistence on habits of sobriety and cleanliness among his workers may sometimes have seemed a little irksome, it also brought some unexpected benefits. It is said that the inhabitants of Saltaire escaped a particularly virulent cholera outbreak that killed many in the surrounding area because they kept out of neighbouring public houses and emptied hot ashes on their privies every night.

Salt did not confine his philanthropic attentions to the village which bore his name. He contributed generously to the rebuilding of York Minister after a fire, to the construction of the Memorial Hall which was erected in London in 1862 to mark the two hundredth anniversary of the birth of English Nonconformity and to numerous mechanics' institutes around the country. He even supplied a lifeboat for Stornoway on the Isle of Lewis. Nearer home, he provided the village of Lightcliffe with a Congregational church, paid for partly out of the proceeds of a lecture on the Holy Land which he gave with coloured photographs 'exhibited by the oxy-hydrogen light' and with the aid of 'persons in oriental costume'. He retained a strong interest in the civic affairs of Bradford and was elected MP for the city in 1859. Although an ardent Liberal and a strong supporter of the principles of free trade and religious equality, he did not enjoy the rough and tumble of political life at Westminster and resigned his seat in the Commons after only two years.

Meanwhile, the business was also demanding his attention. In 1868 he became the first textile manufacturer to produce worsted material for men's suits in place of the traditional all-woollen cloth. This innovation was to help the West Riding worsted industry through a lean time in the late 1870s when the growth of protectionism abroad and the move in women's fashions away from crinolines and towards more figure-hugging dresses combined to depress the lustre trade. More immediately, the expansion of Salt's business, which was now employing around 4,000, necessitated the opening of a new spinning mill. Once again Salt chose an Italianate style of architecture and modelled the factory chimney on the campanile of Santa Maria Gloriosa in Venice.

Titus Salt was much honoured in his lifetime both for his industrial achievements and for his public work and philanthropy. His worsteds were exhibited in the Great Exhibition of 1851 and in the 1861 Paris Exposition where he was presented with the Grand Medal of the Legion of Honour. He was made a baronet in 1869, probably largely at the instigation of Gladstone. An ornate statue of him, surrounded by a Gothic canopy similar to that on the Albert Memorial in London, was unveiled outside Bradford Town Hall in 1874 having been paid for by public subscription. Salt was horrified when he first heard about it, commenting 'so they want to make me into a pillar of salt', and he refused to come to the unveiling ceremony. Had he done so, he would have heard a stirring tribute from fellow-Congregationalist, industrialist and philanthropist Samuel Morley to that remarkable group of Victorians to which both men belonged: 'When the history of England comes to be written, a very substantial chapter will be given to the class of men of whom Sir Titus Salt is a distinguished ornament, and who, by personal sympathy and continuous earnest effort, have contributed so largely to the good work that has been done during the last forty years.'

The last good work that Sir Titus Salt performed on this earth was to open a Congregational Sunday School in Saltaire, with accommodation for about 800 scholars, in May 1876. A few months later he was dead. It was estimated that 120,000 people turned out to witness his last journey from Lightcliffe to Saltaire via the centre of Bradford. There were more than 40,000 in the funeral procession itself and 10,000 lined Victoria Road as the coffin was carried to its final resting place in a special mausoleum adjoining the Congregational church. Work stopped at every mill for miles around on the day of the funeral as Bradford and its satellite villages mourned the man who had made it Worstedopolis.

Sir Titus Salt was a man of almost stark simplicity and straightforwardness who was sustained in everything he did by a deep religious faith and a belief in every individual's capacity for self-improvement. His motto was 'Quid non, Deo Juvante' (With God, nothing is impossible). For all his wealth and his powerful influence over his workforce, he was in some ways a very humble figure. He hardly ever used the special gallery which was built for him above the door of Saltaire Congregational Church, preferring on his visits there to sit with the rest of the congregation in the body of the church. His own tastes were simple – his one personal indulgence was to buy a gold watch when his savings reached £1,000. His favourite pastime in later years was tending his bananas in the greenhouse at Lightcliffe.

In common with many other Nonconformist industrialists of his age, he did, perhaps, display a certain philistinism and lack of

39

cultural interests, as when he replied to a question about what books he read, 'Alpaca – if you had four to five thousand people to provide for every day you would not have much time left for reading'. But he was passionately committed to the extension of education at all levels, believing it to be the route to self-improvement and advancement. He was stern, and to our modern eyes even harsh in his attitudes to his workforce. He employed child labour and opposed legislation raising from eight to ten the age at which children could be employed in factories as 'half-timers'. He had little time for trade unions and none at all for direct industrial action by workers. In 1868 he refused to meet a group of striking weavers who complained that they were not being paid the standard wage for the district, and let it be known that he would only consider their request if and when they returned to work. In 1876 unrest in his mill was met with a lock-out of all workers.

Yet in many ways Salt was a remarkably enlightened employer. His spontaneous acts of generosity to individual workers facing hard times have already been mentioned. His views on the importance of giving his workers a clean and pleasant environment and facilities for education and recreation were far in advance of those of most entrepreneurs of his time, as was his strong advocacy of profit sharing. Unfortunately, he was not able to carry his fellow partners on this last point, but a compromise was reached whereby employees were placed on piece work and so given a direct interest in the products of their labour without any pecuniary risk. Salt was an unashamed paternalist with all the faults which that style of management implies in twentieth-century eyes, but he was not a tyrant. He believed firmly in the essential harmony of interest between capital and labour and felt that the betterment of the lot of the working classes lay within their own hands, to be encouraged by political reforms, education and the cultivation of self-help.

The massive mill at Saltaire which once drew visitors from all over the world as a showpiece of British industry is now an empty and silent monument to the great days of the West Riding worsted industry. It looked at one stage as though it would not survive long after its founder's death. Salt's sons, who took over the business, went bankrupt in 1892 and the company was wound up and restarted by a group of Bradford businessmen. It survived the gradual contraction of the British textile industry which took place in the first half of the twentieth century but has been unable to withstand the more sudden collapse of the last fifteen years. A progressive winding down of operations began in the mid-1970s when wool combing was stopped in the mill. Spinning was abandoned in 1984 and the following year the mill closed down completely with weaving being transferred to another mill in Bradford which, ironically, had been established by one of Titus Salt's great rivals, James Drummond. The trade mark 'Salt's of Saltaire' survives, but the cloth which now bears this famous name is manufactured in one of the most rundown parts of Bradford which is notorious as the city's red-light district.

Saltaire itself has become progressively less of a working community and more and more of a tourist attraction. Most of the original houses remain in good condition although they ceased to be tied to the mill in 1933 when they were sold to a local estate agent, and most are now owner-occupied. The Victorian atmosphere of the village has been heavily promoted by Bradford Metropolitan Council and has played a key role in the city's successful drive to establish itself as a holiday centre. Increasing numbers of visitors come to Saltaire to enjoy its 'quaint' period flavour. The boathouse has been turned into a mock Victorian restaurant with flock wallpaper, potted plants and sepia prints. The institute houses a museum of Victorian reed organs and harmoniums. It has also been fitted with a hideously ugly bar and plays host to meetings of the local wine circle. It is perhaps just as well that when a statue of Sir Titus was erected in 1903 in the park across the river his back was turned on the village and his gaze fixed on the hills to the north. At least there are reliefs of an alpaca and an angora on the base to remind visitors of why the whole place was ever built.

The future of the mill itself is uncertain. It is possible that parts of the former Palace of Industry will be used for small craft workshops. Already a section of the rear of the building houses about a hundred such units. There is also talk of establishing a national museum of industrial history, but Bradford already has two first-class industrial museums and there is a limit to the number of disused factories in Britain which can be turned into reminders of our proud industrial past. Perhaps the most enterprising project being discussed by local businessmen is to convert the office block at the front of the mill into a hotel to cater for Saltaire's growing number of visitors. When so much else that the place originally stood for has been destroyed, it would be nice to think that what they have in mind is a temperance establishment, but somehow I doubt it.

3
SAMUEL MORLEY
(1809–86)

The Old Vic is one of London's most famous theatres, attracting audiences from all over the world for its high-class performances of classic plays. Few probably realize as they take their seats that they owe their evening's entertainment to the vision and generosity of a Victorian manufacturer of stockings and underwear who was also responsible for establishing the first library for children in Britain and for setting up what is now one of the largest adult education centres in the country.

Like Sir Titus Salt, Samuel Morley was an ardent Congregationalist and fervent Liberal who built up the business started by his father into the largest of its kind in the textile industry. Rumoured in his time to be the richest commoner in England, he was simple and even puritanical in his personal habits and tastes and practised practical philanthropy on a grand scale. Unlike Holloway and Salt, he did not commit himself to one or two large projects but chose rather to distribute his bounty far and wide, spending £20,000 to £30,000 a year on a mass of good causes including the YMCA, temperance music halls, Nonconformist churches and the trade union movement of which he was a powerful champion.

The firm of I. & R. Morley was one of the largest industrial and commercial enterprises in Victorian Britain, employing a total of 8,000 people in seven factories in the East Midlands and a large warehouse and office complex in London. Over this vast empire Samuel Morley directly presided, notwithstanding his many other commitments as a Member of Parliament and leading figure in the world of Nonconformity. A remarkably enlightened employer, he

43

took a close personal interest in the welfare of those who worked for him and was like a father to the boys serving apprenticeships in the London counting-house.

Samuel Morley is unique among the enlightened entrepreneurs featured in this book in coming from the south-east of England. He was born in 1809 in Homerton, a district in north-east London favoured by Nonconformist immigrants from the provinces. His father, John, was a former farmer who had come down from Nottingham in 1791 to run the London end of the hosiery business which he had set up with his brother, Richard.

Samuel, who was the youngest of six children, imbibed almost with his mother's milk the vigorous creeds of Nonconformist religion and radical Liberalism which were to sustain him throughout his adult life. His father was an ardent Congregationalist and a no less ardent supporter of the reforming cause in politics, but while making clear his own beliefs he never tried to force his children to follow them. Samuel recalled that he often said to them 'I will tell you why I am a Liberal, and if you think I am right, you can be as I am and do as I do, but you are perfectly free to form your own conclusion'. This broadmindedness was to be a feature of Samuel's outlook as well, although he never for a moment doubted the faith of his father. He grew up as a serious-minded boy without being priggish and his schoolmasters predicted a career either in the pulpit or in politics.

It was, however, into the world of business that Samuel was sent after leaving school. He went into his father's counting-house in Wood Street, near Cheapside in the City of London, while his elder brother, John, went into the firm's warehouse in Nottingham. A third brother, William, later also joined the firm. Samuel showed a natural talent for book-keeping and financial management and quickly became the effective superintendent of the counting-house clerks. He was a shrewd financier, never keeping larger balances standing idle than absolutely necessary and taking advantage of every favourable change in the money market. He worked fast but always very carefully and insisted on the highest standards both from himself and from others. He refused to tolerate sloppy work, no matter who was responsible.

He once angrily rebuked his father for filling in a page of accounts untidily with an old quill pen. One of those who worked with him recalled that 'the ledgers, as soon as he ruled in the counting-house became pictures of neatness and beauty of penmanship'.

Samuel remained in the counting-house for seven years. In 1832 he was transferred to Nottingham to manage a new manufacturing department making flannel underwear. It is not clear whether he himself was behind this important new venture by the firm, which had hitherto concentrated entirely on socks and stockings. Certainly, he was always on the lookout for new commercial ideas and possible new products. But his talents lay in accountancy and finance rather than in factory management and he was soon back in London supervising the work of the counting-house. Initially, he lived above the office in Wood Street, but in 1841 he and his new wife, Rebekah Hope, the daughter of a Liverpool banker, moved to a house in Lower Clapton near his parents' home. His father had retired the previous year and in 1842 his brother William left the business, leaving Samuel effectively running the financial side of the firm. He built up the London end of the business, erecting a new five-storey warehouse and office block on the corner of Wood Street and Gresham Street in 1847 and increasing the City staff from 30 to 100 by 1850.

Samuel Morley had few recreations or pastimes outside his work but he did find time to become actively involved in Nonconformist religious circles. He was a regular attender at the King's Weigh House Congregational Chapel which became known as 'the Nonconformist Cathedral of Wealth' and where fellow worshippers included Jeremiah James Colman of the Norwich mustard firm and Matthew Hodder, founder of the publishing firm Hodder & Stoughton. At this time Nonconformists were protesting about the many unfair burdens which they had to bear, chief among them being the compulsory rates which they were forced to pay towards the upkeep of their local Anglican church. Morley took a leading role in their campaigns and in 1847 he became chairman of the Dissenters' Parliamentary Committee which was set up to promote the election of more Nonconformists to Parliament.

In 1855 Richard Morley died and Samuel's elder brother, John, retired to devote himself to 'Christian usefulness'. Richard's son, Arthur, who had taken over the Nottingham end of the business, died five years later. This left Samuel Morley in sole charge of the family firm. Although his experience and expertise lay almost entirely on the financial side, this did not stop him carrying out a major reorganization and expansion of the manufacturing operation. When he took over, the great bulk of the firm's output was produced by framework knitters working in their own homes. By 1856 Morleys employed more than 2,700 of these domestic outworkers in Nottingham. The knitters paid the firm a rent for their stocking frames and were paid on a piece-work basis, their finished work being collected and brought to the warehouse by middlemen.

Samuel Morley gradually moved the firm towards a system of factory production, taking advantage of recent technological advances to make stockings on power-driven machines. He set up the first factory, employing 500 workers, in Manvers Street, Nottingham, in 1866. The traditional outworkers were by no means dispensed with altogether. Many older framework knitters were kept on until their retirement and were used for sewing and finishing and for quality work like silk stockings. But factory production steadily increased and came to account for the bulk of the firm's output. In keeping with this new mechanized approach, the firm adopted as its trade mark a 'flying wheel' with feathered wings. In all, seven factories were established in the East Midlands in the next twenty-four years. Some concentrated on spinning yarn, some on knitting and others on dyeing and finishing. They supplied a central warehouse in Fletchergate, Nottingham, from where hampers of knitwear were dispatched to the Wood Street warehouse in London. By the end of the 1880s 3,000 workers were employed in the factories, with a further 4,000 indirectly employed as domestic outworkers and over 1,000 in the warehouses and offices.

This expansion was accompanied by a diversification in the firm's products. Hosiery remained the mainstay of Morleys, ranging in quality from rough woollen leggings to fine silk stockings. The stockings which Queen Victoria wore at her coronation in

1837 were made by one of the firm's framework knitters, John Derrick. Fifty years later he made her a pair to wear at her Golden Jubilee. Throughout her reign Victoria was a regular customer of Morleys and her patronage confirmed its reputation as the leading hosiery house in the land. But under Samuel Morley's management the firm also went into the glove-making business and manufactured a wide variety of underwear, including nightdresses, flannel drawers, chamois-leather vests and bodices to be worn under figure-hugging dresses, and an extensive collection of corsets, ranging from the ultra-respectable 'Princess of Wales' and 'Grand Duchess' to the more risqué 'French woven frilly and lacy'. Business boomed as these new lines found a ready market among the fashion-conscious Victorian middle classes. Annual sales rose from £100,000 in 1830 to £1 million in 1859 and reached £2 million in 1871.

One of the reasons for this success was undoubtedly the high quality of both the goods and the service which Morleys offered. Samuel Morley insisted that every article sold should be examined and personally approved and that the slightest flaw should be sufficient to reject it. He also laid down as a principle of the firm that any customer should be able to obtain at any time precisely the same kind of article as he had purchased on any previous occasion. Shoddy workmanship and poor stocktaking were not to be tolerated.

But if he insisted on the highest standards from his workers, he also treated them well. His factories were light, airy and well-ventilated. He paid high wages – a knitter with Morleys received sixpence more per dozen hose than the going rate in the industry generally – and he did not use the hated truck system, common in the textile trade at the time, whereby payment was made in goods or in tokens redeemable only at the company store. Retired employees were paid pensions and special help was given to dispossessed framework knitters. Unlike many other manufacturers, I. & R. Morley did not reduce rates paid to outdoor workers when demand was slack. Indeed, knitters were relieved of paying rents on their frames when they lay idle. But if employees knew that they would not be laid off when trade was slack, they knew also that they would be expected to put in extra hours at busy periods. It was not unknown for packing-room staff at Wood Street to start at 7.15 in the morning and work until midnight when trade was particularly heavy.

Throughout his time as head of the firm Samuel Morley continued to live in London. He appointed a manager, Thomas Hill, to run the Nottingham end of the business and in 1850 took him into partnership. He himself never interfered with the running of the factories. On his visits to the East Midlands he was concerned only with the welfare of the workers and not with technical or production matters in which he had little interest. He did, however, continue to exercise very close supervision over the day-to-day work of the counting-house in Wood Street. This became a hive of activity with the firm's expansion. At one time 2,000 letters were arriving in the first post every day with a further 100 in each succeeding delivery. Only the Prudential Assurance Company handled a larger volume of mail. The House of Morley came to be seen as a first-class training ground for aspiring City clerks and it was the fond hope of many a mother that her son might be accepted as an apprentice there. As one who was lucky enough to start his commercial career with the firm put it, 'A berth in Morley's meant self-respect, honour and emolument, such as no other place in England gave to faithful service'.

Samuel Morley made a point of taking on boys from poor homes as clerical apprentices. He was particularly keen on those from poor Christian homes but in the words of his friend and biographer, Edwin Hodder, 'There was no question raised as to whether they made profession of Christianity – the only question ever put was to ascertain whether they were Protestant, as Mr Morley would not, for the sake of the others, allow a Roman Catholic to come amongst them lest he should – as duty bound – seek to propagate the tenets of his Church'.

Morley demanded from the boy clerks those high standards which had distinguished his own apprenticeship in Wood Street. He insisted on punctuality, neatness, good handwriting and hard work. In return he took a close personal interest in his young apprentices and offered easily the best conditions of employment in London. Most lived in accommodation over the office and had the use of a dining room, parlours and a library and reading room. Penny readings, evening classes and debates were laid on in the evenings, 'cheap and pure literature' was made available and, for those who did not share their employer's teetotal principles, the best beer available was served with meals.

Until 1865, when his election to Parliament made it impossible to continue the practice, Samuel Morley paid each of his clerks personally every week so that he could discuss any matters which they wished to bring up with him. He was particularly concerned with their spiritual development. In 1854 a meeting which he held with the Wood Street apprentices about how best to sustain and extend the spirit of the establishment led to the formation of a Young Men's Christian Association on the premises. Lecturers, like Thomas Binney, who was minister at the King's Weigh House Chapel, and the great Baptist preacher, Charles Spurgeon, came to speak to the young men and missionary and social work was begun in the Barbican district.

Morley was, in fact, one of the leading supporters of the national YMCA movement which had been launched in 1844 by a fellow worshipper at the Weigh House Chapel, George Williams, specifically for young men in the London drapery trade. The two men shared a deep concern about the moral, intellectual and physical well-being of the growing number of young men who were coming to London to take up clerical jobs and agreed on the need to establish associations for them. Morley wrote: 'It is the business of these associations to seek out young men fresh from the influence of pure home life, who find themselves desolate and lonely in London, and to get the earliest possible hold upon them before they form connections which are deteriorating or destructive of morals and personal character.' He served for many years on the executive committee of the YMCA and was one of its main benefactors. In 1880 he made a donation of £5,000 to enable the association to buy Exeter Hall in the Strand for use as a gymnasium and recreation centre.

Morley became renowned as one of the foremost philanthropists in London and received hundreds of letters every year appealing for financial help. He read each request carefully and marked on the top left-hand corner either 'Yes', 'No – litho' (lithograph letter of refusal) or 'Inquire further'. Much of his bounty was directed towards individuals who were down on their luck. He helped many writers and artists through difficult periods, among them George Cruikshank, the cartoonist. He was especially keen to help ministers of religion and teachers suffering hardship or doubts about their vocation. He approached his charitable giving in a businesslike way, always wanting to know where his money was going and not wishing to waste time. He could be peremptory with suitors. One clergyman who had insisted on coming to see him during business hours was told to state his case in five minutes and sent packing when he embarked on a long-winded statement.

In dealing with requests for help from institutions, Morley almost always applied the principle of self-help. He told those churches which appealed to him for funds, 'Whatever you can raise among yourselves, I will make it double'. But he accepted that however carefully he examined requests for help and however much he exhorted those applying for his charity to help themselves, there would inevitably be those among the recipients of his money who were undeserving or fraudulent. He consoled himself with the thought that 'it is better to help a drone than to let a bee perish'.

Although it was spread very widely, Morley's philanthropy was particularly focused on certain areas. He took a special interest in the moral and intellectual elevation of the working and lower middle classes, and the promotion of temperance and Nonconformity. Straightforward Christian evangelism was another favourite cause. He was a strong supporter of the inter-denominational London City Mission, the Salvation Army and the rumbustious missions carried out in the Lambeth public baths by the Revd George Murphy, a Congregational minister. In 1859 he was instrumental in starting Sunday afternoon services in London theatres with the aim of bringing religion to those who would never go to church.

Education was another favourite object for his philanthropy. He was especially keen to promote the higher education of those who, because of their religion or social position, were excluded from the aristocratic and Anglican world of Oxford and Cambridge. In the

1870s he took a leading part in the planning of Cavendish College in Cambridge which was designed to provide a university education for those who came from the commercial middle class. The venture failed but the buildings were subsequently taken over by Homerton College. He gave £2,000 each to the new university colleges at Aberystwyth and Nottingham and generously supported Congregational theological colleges in both England and Wales. He also helped to set up Milton Mount College in Bournemouth as a school for the daughters of Congregational ministers. Nor did he neglect the education and intellectual improvement of the working classes. Discovering in 1881 that the newly opened library in Nottingham was closed to those under fifteen, he established a separate library in the town 'to provide pure and wholesome literature for children'. It was the first children's library in Britain.

Like most Victorian Nonconformists and Liberals, Samuel Morley held strong views about the evils brought about by drink and believed that it lay at the root of many of the social ills of the day. 'Many people begin at the wrong end', he wrote. 'They say people drink because they live in bad dwellings; I say they live in bad dwellings because they drink. It makes all the difference the way you put it. The first essential is not to deal with the habitation, but the habit.' He himself became a total abstainer after addressing a meeting of working men on the evils of drink in 1857. At the end of his speech, a member of the audience got up and asked, 'Do you go without yourself? I dare say, if the truth's known, you take your glass or two of wine after dinner and think no harm of it. Now sir, do you go without yourself?' Morley records in his diary: 'This rather shut me up for an instant but when I looked round at these poor fellows whom I had been asking to give up what they regarded – no matter how erroneously – as their only luxury, I had my answer ready pretty quickly. "No," I said, "but I will go without from this hour."' He was as good as his word. For the last twenty-nine years of his life he did not touch a drop of alcohol and proudly wore the blue ribbon, the badge of total abstainers, on his lapel when in the office, in the House of Commons, at public meetings and at home.

Later, when he went into Parliament, Morley strongly supported legislation designed to curb drinking, like the 1872 Licensing Act, which restricted pub opening hours, and the 1881 Act which prohibited the payment of wages in public houses. Like many Liberals, he campaigned for a system of local option whereby a majority of the inhabitants of a neighbourhood could veto the setting up or continuation of licensed premises there. He also pressed for the ending of commission payments to landlords so that their profits were not 'dependent on the intoxicating drinks which are consumed, but on the cleanliness, comfort, order and accommodation of his house'.

More positively, he believed that the success of the temperance movement depended on providing alternative places of recreation to the ubiquitous public house. He bought a building in central Nottingham which was earmarked to become a gin palace and turned it instead into a club and temperance café for working men, with premises for YMCA and Sunday School meetings. In London he was much involved in a charitable company which hoped to convert the Old Vic Theatre from being one of the capital's most notorious drinking dives into a temperance music hall and coffee tavern. Melodramas and bawdy songs were banished from the theatre in 1880 and in their place was substituted 'entertainment cleansed from objectionable matter and freed from anything of a debasing character'. Unfortunately, but perhaps not surprisingly, this new mixture of attractions proved less popular than the old with the working-class audiences of south London and the company went into liquidation. However, the project was saved when Morley donated £1,000 to start a fund to purchase the lease of the theatre.

He hoped that the Old Vic would become a people's palace putting on attractive entertainments that would woo people from public houses. He told a meeting in 1884, 'Evidence is accumulating as to the conditions of filth, depression and moral ruin in which vast masses of the population of London are living. At our peril we must do something to win them to a better and higher life.' Morley died in 1886, but by 1888 the fund which he had started was large enough for the lease of the theatre to be purchased by Emma

Cons, a Christian socialist who had been instrumental in the earlier abortive attempt to turn it into a coffee tavern. The Old Vic became a combined theatre, temperance hall and adult education centre. Regular evening classes were held, first in the dressing rooms and then in a portion of the building which was named Morley College in memory of Samuel. The theatre became one of the leading classical playhouses in London under the direction of Emma Cons's cousin, Lilian Baylis. It continued to accommodate the adult education classes until 1924 when Morley College moved out to the premises which it still occupies in Westminster Bridge Road.

The world of Nonconformity benefited considerably from Morley's generosity. In the 1860s alone he gave £14,000 towards the building of new chapels around the country. Naturally, he favoured the Congregationalists but he did not limit his gifts to his own particular denomination. The cause of Dissent as a whole appealed to him, and he took a leading part in the celebrations held in 1862 to commemorate the bicentenary of the event normally regarded as marking the beginning of Nonconformity in Britain when 2,000 puritan ministers resigned from their pulpits rather than take the Act of Uniformity. Morley gave £6,000 towards the building of a memorial hall on the site of the old Fleet Prison in Farringdon Street. Known as Morley's Shop, the hall was to achieve a place in history as the birthplace of the Labour Party in 1900.

Morley was also deeply involved in the political struggles of Nonconformists for equal rights with those who belonged to the Established Church of England. He was for many years a keen campaigner for the disestablishment of the Anglican Church although he later modified his views on this subject. It was partly to carry on the struggle for religious freedom and equality that he became an MP. He was also led into a political career by his keenness to see carried into Westminster and Whitehall the principles of efficiency and competition which ruled commercial life. Like other businessmen, Morley was appalled by the slackness and incompetence of many government ministers and civil servants. Lax attitudes which would never be tolerated in the smallest counting-house were the rule in the great departments of state. In 1857 he became chairman of the Administrative Reform Association, set up in the aftermath of the Crimean War by a group of businessmen and reformers who were appalled at the aristocratic amateurism which apparently distinguished the higher reaches of both the Army and the Civil Service. The main aim of the association was to end patronage in these institutions by securing a system of entry by competitive examination and promotion by merit.

Samuel Morley sat in the House of Commons for a total of eighteen years, first as MP for Nottingham from 1865 to 1866 and then representing Bristol from 1868 to 1885. His time in Parliament coincided with the heyday of Gladstonian Liberalism of which he was a fervent supporter. Gladstone's governments brought about many of the reforms for which he had campaigned – the abolition of compulsory church rates and of religious tests at Oxford and Cambridge, the tightening up of drinking laws, the introduction of competitive entry into the Civil Service and the ending of the purchase of commissions in the Army. They also maintained the conditions on which the prosperity of Victorian Britain rested – free trade, non-intervention abroad and sound finance at home. It was small wonder that Morley regarded Gladstone as 'the greatest, purest, and ablest statesman of the present age'.

Throughout his time as an MP, Samuel Morley was seen as the leading representative of Nonconformity in Parliament. He was also regarded as one of the most powerful merchant princes of his day. His influence was considerable, not just in the worlds of religion, politics and industry but more widely, too, through his ownership of one of the main Liberal newspapers, the *Daily News*, which had been founded in 1846 with Charles Dickens as its first editor.

But for all his wealth and power, Morley did not choose to mix with the great and his attitudes were not those of the typical plutocrat. He was a strong supporter of trade unions and of the political aspirations of organized labour. In 1865 he was closely involved in the establishment of the Reform League, a trade union dominated pressure group to secure the vote for working men. Three years later he was instrumental in securing an electoral pact between the League and the Liberal Party. The Lib–Lab alliance which this agreement forged was very dear to Morley's heart. He believed passionately in the harmony of interests between employers and workers and refused to accept that the forces of capital and labour were irreconcilably opposed and bound to come into conflict with the march of industrialization. It was for that reason that he strongly supported the establishment of machinery for conciliation and arbitration in the event of industrial disputes.

Morley had a genuine and deep sympathy with the working classes in their struggle for political and social emancipation. He supported the Chartist demonstrations in the 1840s, gave financial backing to trade union and labour journals and welcomed the formation of the Trades Union Congress in 1868. He happily presided at meetings addressed by speakers of markedly revolutionary tendencies and on one occasion even shared a platform with Karl Marx. When chided for this by other employers he replied: 'It is better that large employers of labour should be willing to hear all that can be said by the advocates of the working class, rather than, from over sensitiveness as to their reputation, or indifference as to the condition of the people, or even fear of "unconscious irony", shut themselves within their own circle.' He himself was far from being a socialist or a revolutionary. But he believed that employers should remain close to their workers, just as he hoped that those workers would themselves rise through education and through their own efforts. He was saddened by the advent of professional trade union negotiators and personnel managers, complaining in 1878: 'There is, I fear, ceasing to be the intimacy between masters and men which existed some years ago. Speaking of my own manufactory, we know scarcely anything of men who have come into our service of late years, because strangers negotiate most of the arrangements which are made.'

As we have seen, Samuel Morley practised what he preached, taking a personal interest in his own workforce and listening to what they had to say. For their part his employees respected and even loved him. When his period as MP for Nottingham came to an abrupt end because of the discovery of certain irregularities among some of his followers, the women in one of his factories in that town worked a number of bookmarks 'bearing upon them encouraging and stimulating passages from Holy Scripture'.

In 1870, at the age of sixty-one, Morley took up residence in Hall Place, a large country house which he had built in the village of Leigh, near Tonbridge in Kent. He effectively became the local lord of the manor, a role which he played with relish, paying for model cottages and almshouses, allotments, a recreation ground and a new system of drainage for the village. Ironically, he also found himself patron of the local parish church with the right and duty to appoint the vicar. He contributed handsomely to repairing the vicarage and the church school and to installing a new organ in the church. But his heart remained with the Nonconformists. One of his first actions on taking up residence in Leigh was to invite an evangelist to hold a series of mission services in a tent in the village. Subsequently he built an independent undenominational chapel. It is now the British Legion Hall. Dr Robert Moffat, the Congregational missionary, was installed in a grace and favour house on the Hall Place estate for the last four years of his life. Morley also extended hospitality to another of his favourite causes. In 1881 a special first-class train brought 350 delegates to an international YMCA conference to take tea on the lawn of his country seat.

Although he assumed the role of country squire, he did not adopt the ways of that breed. His tastes had always been simple, almost puritanical. He enjoyed music and sang ballads with his daughter but violently disapproved of any of his eight children dancing, which he regarded as 'the lust of the flesh, the lust of the eyes and the pride of life'. He did, however, allow himself a smoking room and billiard table at Hall Place. A close friend remarked that 'as to the gaieties of society, or fashionable amusements such as races, theatres, balls, etc., he was either persuaded that they were wrong, and therefore would have nothing to do with them, or he had no taste for them'. He had few relaxations beyond an annual walking tour and an interest in driving horse-drawn phaetons. He read few books. Yet he remained remarkably open-minded and his capacity for interesting himself in new projects was boundless. Wherever he went he carried a black morocco leather bag full of unanswered letters and notes for speeches. He took it out at every opportunity, never wasting a moment when he could be getting on with some useful business.

Samuel Morley's involvement in religious and political causes, and his radicalism, continued unabated until the end of his life. In 1885 he was offered a peerage and had no hesitation in turning it down. Among his public engagements in the months before he died were pledging himself to buy new central premises for the YMCA, giving a lunch to promote Mansfield College in Oxford and speaking at the Lambeth Baths 'with unusual force . . . on the evils of intemperance'. He sent a final public letter to his former constituents in Bristol urging support for Gladstone's Irish Home Rule Bill. He died in September 1886 and was buried in Abney Park Cemetery, North London. His funeral was attended by representatives of more than a hundred religious, social and philanthropic institutions. A group of flower girls whom he had rescued from the streets placed on his grave a floral wreath which they themselves had woven, while some Indian orphans left a tribute 'in sweet memory, with grateful blessing and tears, for our kind and noble sahib'. A plain stone monument records simply 'A friend to Jesus Christ'.

Like Sir Titus Salt, Samuel Morley epitomized the simplicity and straightforwardness of the Nonconformist Conscience. He was quite without guile or pretensions. His attitudes expressed the vigorous individualism of mid-Victorian Liberalism. 'Life', he once reflected, 'is really a continued competitive examination.' He himself, and those like him who were able, hard-working and self-disciplined, passed that examination with flying colours. But he did not despise the weaker brethren who found the competition too tough and fell by the wayside. His spirit was generous and his outlook broad and tolerant.

Both the family and the firm of Morley continued to prosper after Samuel's death. His eldest son, Samuel Hope-Morley, was elevated to the peerage as the first Lord Hollenden. Another son, Arnold, was active in Liberal Party politics and became

Gladstone's chief whip in the Commons. Two other children, Howard and Mary, continued their father's work in the YMCA, and were respectively commemorated in the Morley Hall near Hanover Square and the Morley Rooms for barmaids and waitresses in Regent Street. Hall Place has remained within the family and is now occupied by Samuel's great-grandson, the third Lord Hollenden. I. & R. Morley continued as a leading independent producer of hosiery and underwear until 1968 when they were taken over by Courtaulds. The takeover brought together two giants of the Victorian textile industry. Samuel Courtauld, who had started weaving silk in Essex in the 1820s and went on to achieve prosperity on the basis of producing black crêpe for mourning, was a near contemporary of Samuel Morley, and like him a strong Nonconformist in religion and radical Liberal in politics.

Statues of Samuel Morley were erected shortly after his death in the two towns which he had represented in Parliament. The one in Nottingham met an unfortunate end in 1927 when it fell off the back of a lorry and broke while being moved from Theatre Square to the Arboretum. A bronze bust was subsequently erected at the entrance to the Arboretum. The Bristol statue has fared rather better and is still an imposing sight, standing today just off the city's inner circuit road, at the junction of Horsefair and Union Street. In the words of a journalist present at its erection 'Mr Morley is represented in the attitude he was wont to assume when addressing an assemblage of people, his left foot slightly advanced, his right hand outstretched in a gesture of appeal, his head erect and his left hand grasping the notes of the speech he is supposed to be delivering'. The inscription on the base reads: 'To preserve for their children the memory of the face and form of one who was an example of justice, generosity and public spirit this statue was erected by more than 5,000 citizens of Bristol.'

Morley's name lives on in other ways too. It continues to be found on the labels of several ranges of menswear. At Christ's Hospital school in Sussex the distinctive yellow woollen stockings worn by the students are still known as Morleys. Every week thousands of students come to Morley College in south-east

London to pursue interests ranging from aikido and anthropology to yoga and Yugoslav folk dance. The man who made a fortune out of underwear and gave it away to a host of good causes is not forgotten.

4
GEORGE PALMER
(1818–97)

Countless railway travellers bound for the West of England must have gazed at the great factory complex which until a few years ago dominated the approach to Reading station. But few can have known the worldwide importance of this industrial site which was immortalized in verse more than a hundred years ago:

> On the banks of Kennet's river,
> In Reading's famous town
> Stands a massive pile of buildings
> Of fame and world renown.
>
> Should a stranger ask the business
> Of the place, what may it be?
> Say 'tis the biscuit city
> Of the famous H&P.

Most of the Huntley & Palmers factory has now been pulled down to make way for car parks and light industrial units. Looking at the site today, with just an office block and some outbuildings remaining, it is hard to imagine that it was once the biggest biscuit factory in the world, employing more than 6,000 people, over a quarter of the working population of Reading. The town grew tenfold in the second half of the nineteenth century, very largely as a result of the phenomenal success of this one industry. As one journalist graphically put it, 'Reading is the hub of the industrial south and Huntley and Palmers ginger nuts hold it together'.

Huntley & Palmers was the result of a partnership between two Quakers, Thomas Huntley, who ran a confectioner's shop in

Reading, and George Palmer, a miller and confectioner from Somerset with a passion for all things mechanical. Legend has it that they came to work together quite by chance. In 1841, so the story goes, Palmer was travelling from Taunton to London by stage-coach. Alighting at the Crown Inn in Reading during a stop for a change of horses he caught sight of Huntley's shop across the road. He went in and discovered that Huntley, who was ill, urgently needed a partner to help him in his business. Palmer, who was itching to try out his ideas for the mechanization of the biscuit-making trade, immediately offered his services and never completed his journey to London.

In fact, like so many good tales, the story is apocryphal. George Palmer and Thomas Huntley were well aware of one another's existence before they became business partners in 1841. They were cousins by marriage and they were also both prominent members of the Society of Friends, that close and interlinked brotherhood which produced so many of the founding fathers of great British businesses in the nineteenth century, particularly in the field of biscuit and confectionery manufacture. We will be encountering two more members of the Quaker 'mafia', George Cadbury and Joseph Rowntree, in later chapters of this book. The third great Victorian chocolate maker, Joseph Fry, was another Friend, and so were Huntley and Palmer's main rivals in the biscuit industry, William Jacob (of cream cracker fame) and John Carr of Peek Freans.

Why was it that so many Quakers went into business and did so well? One reason is that many other professions were effectively barred to them because of their religious beliefs. Their pacifism ruled out a career in the armed forces, the legal profession was generally shunned because it involved the administering of oaths and an artistic occupation was regarded as frivolous. In common with other Nonconformists, members of the Society of Friends were unable to study or teach at Oxford and Cambridge. Given these restrictions, it is not surprising to see that so many entered the worlds of commerce and industry. Nor is it surprising that they were often very successful. As George Cadbury put it, 'the training of Friends gave them the qualities most likely to lead to success in business. They were taught self-denial, rigid abstinence from all luxury and self-indulgence.' Quakers were highly self-disciplined and utterly honest. These were important attributes in a world where punctuality in paying creditors and a reputation for financial integrity were considerable commercial assets.

The high standards which the Quakers imposed on themselves go a long way to explaining their particular success in the confectionery and biscuit-making industries. Unlike less scrupulous competitors, their consciences would not allow them to use anything but the purest and best-quality ingredients. In an age when short weight and adulterated foodstuffs were commonplace, and when customers were becoming increasingly discerning about what they ate, the guarantee of absolute purity that every Quaker-made product carried counted for much. It was, indeed, to be the basis on which Rowntrees and Cadburys came to dominate the British chocolate trade and it was also of considerable importance to the success of Huntley & Palmers.

Rather like freemasons today or the Mormons of Salt Lake City, the Victorian Quaker entrepreneurs were part of a tightly knit and mutually supportive community. The extent to which the Society of Friends provided a ready-made and reliable support system for businesses is very clear in the case of Huntley & Palmers. The grocer who supplied the firm with most of their ingredients was a Quaker. So was the ironmonger who made their biscuit tins and the proprietor of the firm which printed their labels. Ties of family were also important. The grocer was related by marriage to George Palmer and the ironmonger was Thomas Huntley's brother. When George Palmer married in 1850 it was to the daughter of a Quaker druggist who was the firm's agent in Basingstoke. This elaborate network of religious and family ties greatly helped the expansion of the firm.

There were, of course, times when the tender consciences of Friends brought them loss rather than profit. They would not pay the compulsory rates which were levied for the upkeep of the local Anglican church and as a result had to face the seizure of goods in lieu. Thomas Huntley had 136 pounds of sugar confiscated on one occasion, while his ironmonger brother, Joseph, was forced to surrender nine kettles and three sets of fire irons. In 1847 Huntley & Palmers had six tins of biscuits worth seventeen shillings seized for non-payment of church rates. Bad debts were another problem that particularly affected Quaker-run firms. Customers took advantage of their patience and gentleness to run up large outstanding bills. Thomas Huntley's business was much afflicted by this problem at the time when he entered into partnership with George Palmer.

Huntley had taken over the shop at 72 London Street, Reading, which his father had started in 1822. Initially most of its business came from travellers waiting to board coaches or stopping for a change of horses at the posting inn opposite. Huntley built up the baking and wholesale side and by the late 1830s he was selling twenty different kinds of biscuit to 117 grocers throughout southern England. Although his turnover was around £2,700 a year, his profits were negligible. In 1841 the business was valued at just over £1,000, of which three-quarters was represented by debts owed by customers. It needed the energy and genius of his new partner, George Palmer, to transform the fortunes of the firm and set it on a course which would make it the biggest and most successful of its kind in the world and one of the forty largest companies in Britain.

George Palmer was born in 1818 in Long Sutton, Somerset. His father, a farmer, died when he was just eight and he was sent to board at Silcot, the Friends' school near Weston-super-Mare. At fourteen he was apprenticed to his uncle who was a miller and confectioner in Taunton. He took a keen interest in the processes of biscuit making, which was at that time carried on entirely by hand. One day while in Bath he bought a packet of Huntley's biscuits and was much impressed by their quality. It may perhaps have been then that George Palmer first conceived the idea of joining his cousin. As one would expect from an arrangement between Quakers, the details of their partnership were very precisely worked out. Huntley was to be the senior partner, keeping the accounts and ledgers and supervising the packing department. Palmer was to manage the manufacturing department and look after sales and correspondence. Each of the two partners was to put £550 into the firm. It was on that basis that George Palmer came to Reading in 1841.

Thomas Huntley conducted his business in one small and cramped building. The only machinery on the premises was a hand-operated roller through which strips of dough were passed to be stamped and cut prior to being baked and sold as Jamaica biscuits. It was still in use in 1939 and is now on display in Reading Museum. His new partner was determined that the factory should be extended and a degree of mechanization introduced into the production process. As a first step he leased a building adjoining the London Street shop and installed steam-driven machinery. Palmer also started advertising in the press. In 1844 a small notice in *The Times* reminded readers that the firm's 'superior' biscuits were sold 'in London and the principal towns of the country by respectable grocers and Italian warehousemen'. Another advertisement spoke of 'the great satisfaction which these biscuits have given in the fashionable watering places, and other towns where they have been introduced'.

To counter the continuing problem of bad debts, George Palmer engaged eight agents to work on a commission basis getting orders from shops and collecting unpaid accounts. He also extended the firm's range of products, adding to popular biscuit lines like Olivers and Macaroons an unfermented bread made with hydrochloric acid and carbonate of soda instead of yeast according to the recipe of a celebrated doctor. By 1845 sixteen people were employed, sales and profits were rising and Palmer felt that the time had come when he could test his ideas for putting biscuit production on a fully mechanized basis. The following year he bought a disused silk mill in King's Road, ideally placed between the River Kennet and the Kennet and Avon canal and adjoining the tracks of Brunel's Great Western Railway which had come to Reading sixteen years earlier.

With the assistance of an engineer, William Exall, George Palmer devised and installed in the new factory the world's first continuously running machinery for biscuit manufacture. Chutes conveyed flour from an upper floor store room into large mixing machines where other ingredients like water, milk, eggs, sugar and treacle were added by hand. The resulting dough was taken to rolling machines through which it passed several times. It was then carried on a canvas conveyor belt to the machines which cut out the shapes of individual biscuits. Spare dough fell into a trough where it was collected for re-use. The biscuits dropped off the belt into trays which were held in place by boys standing in pits below floor level. Other boys collected the trays and stacked them on trolleys to be taken to the ovens. When they were baked the trays of biscuits were taken by a lift known as 'Jacob's ladder' to the second storey of the factory where they were sorted out. Imperfect biscuits were broken up by a special machine and a pound of the resulting pieces was given to each employee every week. The perfect biscuits were stored in casks to await packaging in tins or boxes.

Initially it looked as though these efforts at mechanization might be over-ambitious. When the first of the seven steam coils which heated the ovens was heated up it exploded, nearly killing George Palmer and others standing nearby. The cost of the new machinery was over £1,000 and, with increased rates and mortgage interest payments on the new premises, there was little left in the way of profits. The factory opened in November 1846 and during the next twelve months the two partners drew only £190 and Huntley complained that his impetuous young associate was well on the way to ruining them both by his passion for innovation.

In fact, once the teething troubles had been sorted out Palmer's introduction of factory mass production more than proved its worth in terms of increased sales. By the end of 1846 Huntley & Palmers were employing 45 workers and supplying 717 retailers, including the prestigious Fortnum & Masons. In 1849 Palmer appointed Henry Lea, another Quaker, as the firm's first full-time commercial traveller. The following year he brought in his brother, Samuel, to supervise sales and in 1851 he made his other brother, William Isaac, factory manager. At the same time he continued his programme of mechanization, introducing travelling revolving ovens which could be loaded directly from the conveyor belt and which could bake different biscuits for varying periods of time.

By 1856 the number of employees was over 350, turnover was more than £105,000 and profits were over £12,000. The following year Thomas Huntley, who had been in increasingly poor health and had for some time been a very inactive partner in the firm, died. Although it kept Huntley in the company name, the business now became effectively a Palmer family firm. Huntley's son, Henry, who had no desire to follow his father, sold his interest in the business and bought a landed estate in Dorset. George Palmer brought his two brothers into partnership and together they ran the firm, henceforth known as Huntley & Palmers. By 1860 there were 500 employees in what had become the largest biscuit makers in England with an output of 3,200 tons a year.

The spectacular growth of Huntley & Palmers' trade was a reflection of the general rise in living standards during the mid-Victorian economic boom. As the purchasing power of all sections of society increased many items which had previously been regarded as luxuries became standard purchases in the weekly household shopping. The biscuit trade was given a boost by other more specific factors as well. The repeal of the Corn Laws in the same year that George Palmer's new automated factory opened allowed cheap wheat into Britain from the grain-growing lands of Eastern Europe, and later from the American prairies. As a result the price of flour fell and biscuits came within the reach of many who were previously unable to afford them. Changing eating habits also played a part. As the middle classes came to eat dinner later in the evening, the great British institution of afternoon tea was born and with it the demand for sweet biscuits and fancy cakes.

Until the middle of the nineteenth century most of the biscuits made in Britain were of a distinctly plain and dry variety. The main brands were called Captain, Water and Cabin and, as the names suggest, they owed much to the traditional ship's biscuit. There is a good example in Reading Museum of one of these plain biscuits, manufactured in 1847 in the new Huntley & Palmers factory and kept in its wrapper until 1939 – it is not a very appetizing sight. But in response to the changing demands of the market, and the growth of the British sweet tooth (helped by the abolition of duties on sugar and tropical fruits), new sweeter and more fancy varieties were produced, among them Ginger Nuts, Digestives, Osbornes, Abernethys and the Pic-Nic and Raspberry biscuits which were taken with a glass of wine and popular at fashionable evening parties. By 1865 Huntley & Palmers were producing 100 different varieties of biscuit.

Another important boost to the biscuit business came from the development of railway travel. Restaurant and buffet cars were not common on trains until late on in the nineteenth century and many travellers found that a packet of biscuits was the ideal snack to take with them on a long journey. Huntley & Palmers had the bright idea of handing every first-class passenger at Paddington Station a packet of their biscuits with instructions on the packet to look out for their factory beside the line at Reading. The company was, in fact, very clever in establishing what would nowadays be called an up-market brand image. As early as the 1850s it was supplying biscuits to Queen Victoria although it was not until 1884 that a royal warrant was granted. In 1867 the firm got warrants from both Napoleon III of France and Leopold II of Belgium and much was made in the same year of the Empress Eugénie's demand for constant supplies at all her royal palaces.

Marketing was one of the areas in which George Palmer's flair and readiness to innovate was most successfully applied. Very soon after becoming a partner, he set up a network of commission agents covering the whole of the British Isles. They were later replaced by a team of commercial travellers who made extensive use of advertising gimmicks like showcards and highly decorated calendars and almanacks. Huntley & Palmers' famous trade mark of the garter and the buckle, still in use today, was first used in 1851 and was one of the first to be registered when the official register of trade marks was introduced in 1876.

Huntley & Palmers' most significant innovation in marketing lay in the field of packaging. The company pioneered the use of the decorative tins which are now so sought after by collectors of Victoriana. As early as 1832 Joseph Huntley was making tins in his ironmonger's shop for his father's biscuit business across the road. In 1846 he went into partnership with his nephew, Joseph Boorne, and in 1872 they were joined by a third Quaker, Samuel Beavan Stevens. The firm of Huntley, Boorne & Stevens is still based in Reading and continues to make biscuit tins today. Originally the tins in which Huntley & Palmers' biscuits were sold had paper labels. In 1868 the company put on sale the first example in Britain of a tin directly printed in full colour. Known as 'The Casket', it was produced by a process of transfer printing developed by Benjamin George in London and manufactured in Reading by Huntley & Boorne.

Although transfer printing represented a major advance, it could only be used on flat surfaces. In 1875, however, Robert Barclay patented a technique of offset litho printing on tin which enabled designs and pictures to appear on curved surfaces. The patent was sold to Bryant & May, the Quaker match manufacturers, who in turn gave Huntley, Boorne & Stevens exclusive rights to practise the technique in Britain. In 1877 Joseph Huntley and his colleagues established 'The Great Lithographic Tin Printing Press' and two years later they produced the first decorated tins using the new process for Huntley & Palmers. Biscuit tins no longer had to be rectangular – circular, triangular and heart-shaped containers started appearing, all embellished with colourful designs and pictures. Early in the 1880s Huntley & Palmers introduced specially decorated tins of assorted biscuits aimed at the Christmas trade. Examples of these ornate containers, which were on occasion shaped to resemble trains, boats and other objects, can be seen in the Reading Museum and in a special collection at Manderston, the Berwickshire home of Adrian Palmer.

Although the majority of their sales were in Britain, Huntley & Palmers built up a sizeable export trade. As early as 1844 the firm had advertised 'biscuits packed in cases of all sizes for families residing in the country and for exportation'. In 1866 George Palmer took on as Continental agent Joseph Leete, who also acted for Crosse & Blackwell's pickles and sauces and Horniman's tea. Leete rapidly built up sales in France by bold salesmanship, organizing a blind tasting of biscuits at the leading Paris food emporium as a result of which the proprietor switched his suppliers from Peek Freans to Huntley & Palmers. He also secured for the Reading firm exclusive rights to supply biscuits to twenty-one of the most important restaurants in the French capital.

Huntley & Palmers established their international reputation at the Great Exhibition in Paris in 1867. They made a special exhibition biscuit which they named the Napoleon and packed in tins decorated with the French tricolour. These were handed out to visitors, as was a sponge rusk said to 'stir champagne without breaking'. Together with Crosse & Blackwell and the Burton-on-Trent brewer, M.T.Bass, Huntley & Palmers dominated the British Food Court at the exhibition and greatly impressed the French by the quality and the price of their products. The journal *Public Opinion* gleefully reported: 'The striking part of this manufacture is that the French cannot compete with the English biscuit makers. That which the French made by hand, the English can do with machinery. At Reading nearly everything is done by machinery. The flour goes in at one end of the series of machines and comes out at the other a perfect Albert.'

By the late 1870s Huntley & Palmers were exporting over £300,000 worth of biscuits a year, or around 30 per cent of their total sales. The largest single overseas market was France where the firm had won the gold medal at the 1878 Paris Exhibition. Biscuits from Reading were also finding their way into the remoter corners of the British Empire and beyond – a British officer taking part in the Afghan Wars was amazed when a captured chief offered him, in broken English, a 'Huntley-Palmer biscuit'. There was also a sizeable traffic across the Atlantic. In 1888 the company appointed as agent William Kennedy, a Quaker who already acted for Rowntrees and who was instructed to 'get into the American cities and watering places first instead of the Wild West'.

The steady increase in sales both at home and abroad led to considerable expansion of the Reading works. In 1857 George Palmer extended the original building and put up a new four-storey factory on the site of an old tobacco works. In 1873 a new manufacturing department was opened at Blake's Wharf on the north bank of the River Kennet. Its opening was celebrated by a party at which 4,000 guests listened to scientific lectures, watched juggling displays and danced to a temperance band. By now Huntley & Palmers' annual requirements included more than 10,000 tons of flour, 2,350 tons of sugar, 1,100 tons of butter, more than 8 million eggs and 270,000 gallons of milk. The workforce of 2,500 embraced not only bakers, labourers and packagers but also carpenters and coopers to make the casks in which the biscuits were stored, painters, plumbers and engineers to look after the plant and machinery, and engine drivers, shunters and signalmen to operate the rapidly growing network of private sidings off the main Great Western railway line. Nearly all the employees were male (2,430 against only 70 women) and around half were under the age of eighteen. Boys were used particularly for fetching and carrying in the bakery and for packaging duties upstairs.

Conditions in the factory were hard. The working day began at 6.30 in the morning and ended at 6.30 in the evening, with forty minutes off for breakfast and an hour for dinner. On Saturdays work finished at 2 p.m. During busy periods this 58½-hour week was often extended by overtime and it was not uncommon for work to go on until 11 p.m. In 1872 the standard working week was reduced to 54 hours. No paid holidays were given and it was not until 1873 that the workers were paid for Christmas Day. Wages were generally low – throughout the nineteenth century flour accounted for around a third of the firm's total costs and wages for less than a tenth. Although there were standard rates of pay, the partners, and later their managers, went through the wage books twice a year and decided whether to raise, leave unchanged or reduce the remuneration of each individual employee. Calls for a more uniform system and for rises in wages were firmly resisted.

In conformity with their Quaker consciences, Thomas Huntley and George Palmer had laid down strict rules of conduct for their employees. Using profane language, striking anyone, or injuring any machine through 'wantonness and neglect' were to be punished with a one shilling fine – a sizeable amount when the average daily wage for men was between three and four shillings. Absence without leave, smoking or bringing liquor into the factory incurred a fine of sixpence, while lesser offences like wasting time or being at work with hands or face unwashed were penalized with a twopenny fine. Rigorous standards of hygiene were enforced – all workers had to wear white aprons and some kind of headgear – and absolute propriety was maintained with male and female employees being required to enter and leave the factory by different gates and at different times.

But although the Quaker regime was stern, it was also tempered with mercy and kindness. George Palmer refused to dismiss employees who had committed offences against the company code of conduct. Although a strict teetotaller himself, he allowed beer to the labourers engaged in building work on the factory site. The fines collected from those who broke the company rules did not go into the partners' pockets but into a sick fund which had been set up in 1849 with George Palmer as president and Thomas Huntley as treasurer. All adult employees contributed sixpence a week to the fund and in return obtained twelve shillings a week when they were sick. For boys the respective rates were one penny and two shillings. Those who could afford it paid one shilling for a consultation with the doctor while others could get a free voucher from the counting-house. The sick scheme, which was supported out of the personal funds of the partners, was administered by a committee of six employees who kept a careful check on any abuses. No one receiving benefit was allowed to travel more than two miles from home and the employee who lived nearest to him was required to call in once a week to check that there was no malingering. On several occasions the partners stepped in with a donation of their own when they felt that the committee had been over-hasty in cutting an individual's benefit.

The sick fund was just one of many welfare schemes which George Palmer introduced for the benefit of his employees. In 1854 he set up a mutual improvement society, also under the democratic control of the workers, with a library and reading room. The partners agreed to pay half the cost of a number of periodicals ranging from *The Times* to *Good Words*, and all employees over the age of sixteen were able to use the rooms on payment of a penny a week. Lectures were organized and William Isaac Palmer installed a piano in the reading room and organized Saturday evening entertainments in an attempt to wean people away from public houses.

In 1868 George Palmer set up a penny bank to encourage thrift and three years later John Holder, one of the earliest employees, was appointed sick visitor and temperance missionary. The partners bought part of the disused Reading racecourse to provide a cricket pitch and athletic ground. Nor were employees forgotten when they retired. A contributory pension scheme was established while those who had worked for the company for more than fifty years received a non-contributory pension. The firm also provided a funeral for every employee who died in service, the cost depending on his status – £7 for a pastrycook, £17 for an engineer and £38 for a foreman.

Days off on full pay were given to celebrate major events in the family life of the partners and important occasions in the history of the firm, like the opening of a new factory or the award of an international prize. George Palmer's marriage to Elizabeth Meteyard in 1850 – a fertile partnership which was to produce ten children – was marked by a special supper; afterwards the employees were entertained to a lecture on the wonders of electricity during which some of the boys were given a mild electric shock. In 1872 the entire workforce was invited to George's home for a party to celebrate the twenty-first birthday of his son, George William. The host began his speech 'Ladies and Gentlemen and fellow co-operatives of the Reading biscuit factory', an indication of the extent to which he saw his workforce as members of an extended family. His view of his employees as partners did not, however, extend to introducing profit-sharing or co-ownership schemes. At heart he was a paternalist and he viewed his workers much as a stern but kindly Victorian father viewed his children. Words of moral exhortation and advice were never far from his lips. When he was addressing the annual tea and social gathering of the firm's cricket club in 1891, for example, he could not resist the opportunity of reminding them that 'there were other duties besides cricket' and encouraging them to take an interest in both science and the arts.

Excursions were an important and popular feature of the life of the firm. Several trips were made to the Crystal Palace in the 1850s and in 1862 there was a special outing to the London International Exhibition after the firm had won a bronze medal for biscuits. In the summer 'aquatic excursions' were held on steamers on the Thames.

72

George Palmer always appeared at tea time and afterwards the Temperance Band played for singing and dancing on the decks. In 1872 the partners decided to provide one day's paid holiday in June. An excursion fund was set up under the management of the Reading Room Committee and employees voted on where they should go. The seaside resorts of Portsmouth, Hastings and Ramsgate were especially popular and once every year up to 7,000 workers would descend on one of these towns, brought there by a fleet of ten special trains from Reading station. Unlike certain other company excursions, Huntley & Palmers' day trips were almost always orderly and without incident, perhaps largely because the partners forbade the carrying of any alcoholic drink.

George Palmer did not confine his philanthropic attentions to his own workforce but also played an important role in civic affairs. His first public office, assumed in the late 1840s, was as secretary to the Reading Boys' School which had been set up in 1810 to teach boys of all social and religious backgrounds. He was concerned about the large number of destitute children who roamed the town's streets and missed out on education, and he took the initiative in setting up a ragged school to cater for such waifs and strays. In addition to lessons, the school offered the attractions of soup and a meal of porridge every day as well as bathing facilities.

In 1850 George Palmer was elected to Reading Town Council. A strong Liberal, he was on the radical reforming wing of the party and keen on social improvement. His first concern was with the public health of the town and the provision of a proper system of drains and sewerage. He was well aware of the problem since an open gutter into which raw sewage and rubbish was discharged ran past the front of Thomas Huntley's original premises in London Street. Palmer complained that when he attempted to wash away the accumulated filth in front of the shop the Reading Water Company complained about the waste of water. Soon after his election to the council he joined the newly formed Board of Health and took a leading role in planning a comprehensive main drainage system and slum clearance programme which did much to rid the town centre of the scourge of cholera and typhoid.

Joined in the running of the firm by his two brothers in 1857, he was able to devote more time to civic affairs and in that year he became mayor of Reading. Education continued to be a major interest and in 1870 he persuaded the town council to put into effect W. E. Forster's famous Education Act to bring elementary schooling within reach of every child. He was made vice-chairman of the local school board that was set up and gave £500 to build Reading School.

In 1878 Palmer was asked to stand for election to Parliament. He was reluctant to be a candidate, being already sixty and having a naturally rather shy disposition, but was finally persuaded to stand by the veteran Quaker MP, John Bright. His manifesto dwelt on the benefits of a peaceful foreign policy and criticized the Conservative Prime Minister, Disraeli, for his jingoistic sabre rattling over the Eastern Question. Duly elected as MP for Reading, he made his maiden speech in the Commons in favour of giving the vote to women – a subject on which he later changed his mind – but spoke seldom thereafter and earned the title of 'the silent member'. He thankfully withdrew from Westminster in 1885. He was subsequently offered a baronetcy but turned it down, saying 'I could not sustain the position it entails with comfort and satisfaction to myself'.

George Palmer's greatest gift to the town of Reading was the provision of parks. Like Salt, he saw the need for open spaces and fresh air in Britain's rapidly expanding and overcrowded industrial communities. As a town councillor, he instigated a policy of purchasing public recreation grounds. In 1876 he himself presented 14 acres of land on King's Meadow to the town and in 1889 he made a further gift of 49 acres for football and cricket grounds and tennis courts. His only condition was that no intoxicating liquor should be sold in what was to become known as Palmer Park. As a token of thanks for this gift, 4,000 citizens of Reading subscribed to erect a statue of George Palmer and the town council voted to make him the first honorary freeman of the borough. The freedom of the town was conferred and the statue unveiled on the same day in November 1891 on which he opened Palmer Park with a characteristic speech pointing out that 'play in the right proportions is as much a moral duty as work'. In the evening a portrait of him in fireworks was illuminated, surrounded by the motto 'The town thanks you'.

The fortunes of the firm still claimed much of George Palmer's time and attention. By now Huntley & Palmers were firmly established as the largest and most famous biscuit makers in the world, employing over 4,000 workers and turning out nearly 400 different varieties at the rate of over 400 tons a week. In 1890–91 turnover was £1.3 million and profits over £200,000. New varieties were constantly being added, ranging from the high-class (Boudoir and Soirée) to the plebeian (Knobble, Tops and Bottoms, and Nic Nac), and from the exotic (Fiji, Java and Jou-Jou) to the distinctly plain (Arrowroot and Meat Wafers). Despite the vast size of the operation, there was still room for the homely touch. In 1884 the firm introduced Honey Drops on the suggestion of a country clergyman who was secretary of the Berkshire Beekeepers' Association and proudly advertised that 'these biscuits have been made to meet the views of benevolent persons who are anxious to create markets for honey produced in cottage gardens'.

The fame of the Reading biscuit works had spread far and wide. They were visited by Ulysses Grant, former president of the United States, in 1877 and by the Empress Eugénie in 1885. By 1890 Huntley & Palmers were making four-fifths of all biscuits exported from Britain. Many of them found their way to the remoter corners of the British Empire. The king of Barotseland, the area around the Zambesi valley that is now the south-east region of Zambia, was fond of finishing his midday meal with tea, native beer and some Huntley & Palmers biscuits. The American journalist Henry Stanley fortified himself with Reading biscuits on his famous trek across Africa to find Dr Livingstone and was once able to pacify a potentially hostile tribe at Suna, in modern-day Tanzania, by giving them some Huntley & Palmers tins.

The tins were, indeed, much more prized in many places than their contents. British soldiers fighting in the Sudan in the early 1880s captured native swords which had scabbards made from metal strips clearly displaying the garter and buckle trade mark. In 1890 two Reading biscuit tins were discovered being used as ornaments on an altar in a tiny Catholic church in Ceylon, while a

Mongolian chieftainess was said to keep one in which she grew garlic heads for flavouring stew 'as an outward and visible sign of her high position'. In Uganda the tins were used as containers for Bibles and prayer books to protect them from ants. Perhaps the most bizarre recorded use of Huntley & Palmers tins was as a makeshift coffin for Prince Henry of Battenberg, the husband of Queen Victoria's youngest daughter, Beatrice. He contracted fever while fighting the Ashanti in West Africa in 1896 and died on the boat home, his body being pickled in rum and placed in a casket made out of the containers of the accumulated ship's rations.

At home, Huntley & Palmers had become a national institution. The Quaker firm even received an episcopal blessing when the Bishop of Oxford welcomed delegates to the Church Congress held in Reading in 1883 by telling them that the prosperity of the town in which they were meeting was based on a product which 'has the savour of the quiet fireside and of the social board'. His comment prompted a leading article in *The Times* and a cartoon in *Punch* of the 'Reading Biscuit Bishop' emerging like a jack-in-the-box from a Huntley & Palmers tin. Two years later the firm achieved the ultimate accolade of being immortalized in a nonsense rhyme by the great Edward Lear:

> Huntley and Palmer arose
> With the earlyful beams of the morning sun.
> Huntley a chop for his breakfast chose,
> Palmer preferred a bun.

Like Holloway's pills, the Reading biscuits had their imitators and the firm was constantly fighting off counterfeiters. In 1893 it went to the High Court to obtain an injunction against a small bakery which was using the name 'Reading' for its biscuits. Affidavits from customers ranging from small provincial grocers to Harrods and Fortnum & Masons were read out testifying that Huntley & Palmers' products were universally known as Reading biscuits. George Palmer recalled that as an apprentice nearly sixty years before he had bought Thomas Huntley's 'Reading biscuits' in Bristol and that when their partnership had started their products were referred to jokingly in Oxford and Cambridge as 'reading biscuits'. The firm won its case.

In the same year as this successful High Court action William Isaac Palmer died. Like his elder brother, he had been a generous philanthropist and active participant in many aspects of local life. Altogether it is estimated that he gave away about £10,000 and his house was besieged every morning by a small crowd seeking aid and advice. He was particularly keen on temperance and claimed that a quarter of the population of Reading had taken the pledge and become teetotallers. William Isaac's death greatly affected George, who received a further blow the following year in the death of his wife. He himself was afflicted by increasing deafness, and although he still went down to the factory every day he was happy to leave much of the running of the firm to Samuel and to the seven second-generation Palmers who were now involved with the company. Following a slight stroke in 1895, George offered Samuel his resignation but this was declined and he remained an active partner of the firm until his death.

George Palmer's last months on earth were filled with the philanthropic activity to which he had devoted much of his life. As a memorial to William Isaac, he donated a site for a museum and art gallery in Reading. In May 1897 he celebrated Queen victoria's Diamond Jubilee by making a personal gift of £7,000 to the Royal Berkshire Hospital and granting a day's holiday on full pay to each of his 5,500 employees. He also gave fifty guineas for the town's civic festivities. On 21 August he died, just a few months short of his eightieth birthday. The five hundred men who had been with the firm for more than twenty years walked behind his coffin as it was carried from his home to the Friends' Burial Ground where he was laid to rest just a few feet away from the grave of Thomas Huntley. The other 5,000 employees lined the route. A letter from sixty members of the Reading workforce spoke on behalf of all when it said 'In Mr George Palmer we have always felt that we had a personal friend'.

It was probably true to say that George Palmer was respected rather than loved by his employees. In some ways he was a harsh employer. As we have already observed, he paid low wages and did not take kindly to requests from his workers for increases. It is said that he once threatened to throw out of his office two employees who had come to ask for a wage rise. But if he was sternly paternalistic in the way he ran his firm, he was also generous almost to a fault in his response to appeals for help from those in need. His habit of bestowing half-crowns indiscriminately on mendicants was said to have turned Reading into the haunt of beggars from all over the country. In the words of a local paper, 'His purse was ever open to the calls of suffering humanity and the promotion of social and religious advancement'.

In the fifty-six years that he lived in Reading, the town's population went up from around 15,000 to 65,000. It is not too much to say that most of that increase was attributable to the astonishing success of the company which George Palmer was largely responsible for building up and which he made one of the best-known names in British industry. He might well have been excused for taking on some of the trappings of a successful merchant prince but instead he remained faithful throughout his life to the Quaker principles of plain living and simplicity. His home in Reading, the Acacias in London Road, was a modest villa from which he walked to work every day. It is true that he owned nearly 3,000 acres of land in Berkshire and Surrey but he leased much of it in the form of allotments and smallholdings and did not maintain a country seat. He kept a small town house in Grosvenor Street but shunned the world of fashionable London society.

Following George Palmer's death Huntley & Palmers became a limited liability company with a share capital of £2.4 million. Three of George's sons and four of Samuel's served as directors but the firm ceased to be quite the close-knit family concern that it had been under the first generation of partners. It also faced increasing competition from other manufacturers and from the new grocery chains which were starting to make their own cheap biscuits. The twentieth century has seen a succession of mergers as the firm has become part of ever bigger conglomerates. The first of these took place in 1921 when it joined with Peek Freans to form Associated Biscuit Manufacturers. Then in 1960 W. & R. Jacob were incorporated in what became Associated Biscuits Ltd.

It is appropriate that these three firms should have come together since they shared common Quaker origins. Peek Freans began in 1857, the year of Thomas Huntley's death, when James Peek, a retired tea merchant, and George Frean, a West Country miller and ship's biscuit maker, set up a factory in Bermondsey. Five years later they were joined by John Carr, from the famous Carlisle biscuit family, who persuaded them to forsake ship's biscuits and concentrate on the more lucrative fancy biscuit trade. William Jacob had begun making fancy biscuits in Waterford, Southern Ireland, in 1850. He later moved to Dublin and it was there in 1885 that he first manufactured the cream cracker with which the name Jacobs has been associated ever since.

Sadly, Reading is no longer 'biscuit city'. Production stopped at the King's Road factory in 1977 and five years later Associated Biscuits were taken over by the giant American firm, Nabisco. In 1985 a further merger took place between Nabisco and another American company, R.J. Reynolds. But the UK headquarters of the group remains at King's Road and the name Huntley & Palmers is still used as a sign of quality on twelve varieties of biscuit, ranging from Digestives and Sponge Fingers to Dutch Shortcake and Chocolate Chip Cookies.

The tangible memorial of George Palmer's great industry and commercial drive may no longer be there for railway travellers through Reading to see, but one result of his philanthropy is easily visible to those who go by motorway. At the end of the M239 spur which links the town with the M4 stands Palmer Park and in the middle of it is the statue of Palmer, transplanted from its original site in the town centre and surrounded by the sports fields which he gave to the town and which are still in daily use. He stands every inch the stern and simple Quaker, bearded, erect and with a top hat and umbrella in his hand.

5

JEREMIAH JAMES COLMAN
(1830–98)

Few products are so firmly linked in the public mind with a single manufacturer's name as mustard is with Colman's. Ask in any British home for some of that fiery condiment and the chances are that out of the sideboard will be produced a tin, a jar or a tube with the familiar yellow label and the bull's head trade mark.

One man played a large part in making the name Colmans synonymous with mustard throughout the British Empire. Jeremiah James Colman moved the firm to the site that it still occupies at Carrow on the outskirts of Norwich and presided over its fortunes for a period of forty-four years during which the number of employees increased from 200 to over 3,000. Through a combination of hard work, good management and skilful delegation he built up a remarkably successful business that continues to this day. Standing more than 6 feet tall and adorned in his later years with a flowing white beard, he struck many who met him as resembling an Old Testament prophet. During his twenty-four years in the House of Commons he was generally regarded as the leading spokesman of the stern and unbending Nonconformist Conscience. To his workforce and to the inhabitants of Norwich, however, he was a kind employer and generous benefactor.

Like Titus Salt and Samuel Morley, Jeremiah James Colman was not a self-made man but joined an existing family business which he then transformed. In his case the business had been started in 1804 by his great-uncle, also called Jeremiah, who had bought a flour mill on the outskirts of Norwich. Ten years later old Jeremiah, as he was known, moved to the village of Stoke Holy Cross, about four miles from the city, where he took over a larger water-powered mill which had been used for paper making and also for the production of flour and mustard. It was there in 1823 that he founded the firm of J.&J.Colman, having taken his nephew, James, Jeremiah James's father, into partnership.

Jeremiah James Colman was born at Stoke in 1830 and grew up in a house opposite the mill. As a boy he was very interested in both music and botany, passions that he was to retain for the rest of his life. He was very serious minded, getting up at 6.30 every morning to begin his studies and joining the Norwich Young Men's Mutual Improvement Society. A devout attender at St Mary's Baptist Chapel in Norwich, he took a leading part in the Sunday School to which he contributed a paper on 'the effect of sin in destroying man's relation to God and his own compound nature'.

At the age of seventeen he joined the family milling business which was still very small and relatively primitive. The first steam machine had only been installed two years earlier and many operations were still carried out by hand. From the start, Jeremiah seems to have taken a strong interest in the technical side of the business. As well as milling flour and mustard, his father and great-uncle were also experimenting with making starch, at first principally from wheat, but also from potatoes and even from chestnuts. Later rice was to become the main raw material for starch production. Jeremiah James took a keen interest in these experiments and carried out some of his own into the production of various kinds of gum which might have similar properties to starch as a stiffener for linen and cotton fabrics. In 1849 he noted in his diary: 'Got home a new galvanic battery from E.Arnolds, to perform some experiments with respect of the gum.'

In 1851 Jeremiah James became a partner of the firm on the death of his great-uncle. Three years later his father died and he was left in sole charge of the manufacturing side of the business with two uncles, Jeremiah and Edward, running the office which had recently been opened in Cannon Street in the City of London. He committed a characteristically earnest entry to his diary as he contemplated the responsibilities that lay ahead:

Standing at the head of a business such as ours is not always smooth work. I know 'tis a perilous position for me to be at so young an age, master absolutely and unreservedly over so many people, and sometimes to have to demand an implicit though be it reluctant obedience.

In one respect, Jeremiah James's task was less daunting than it might have been since one critical decision had already been taken before he became sole resident partner at Stoke. This was to move the entire manufacturing operation to a site nearer Norwich. It was quite clear that the firm had outgrown Stoke. There were now nearly 200 people employed in milling, blending and packaging mustard, flour and starch and most had to make the four-mile journey from Norwich, which meant them getting up at 4.30 to be at work by 6 a.m. and not getting home again until 7.30 p.m. The Stoke works were badly situated for communications, being four miles from a navigable waterway and two miles from the nearest station on the recently opened Eastern Counties Railway. As a result flour and mustard seed had to be brought in by waggon and the same method of transport used for carting goods to customers in London and elsewhere.

In 1850 J. & J. Colman had bought land belonging to the Norfolk Railway Company at Carrow on the southern outskirts of Norwich. This site had the advantage of excellent communications, being adjacent to the main railway line from London and to the River Wensum which, when joined by the River Yare just east of the site, offered a direct link to the coastal port of Great Yarmouth. Carrow had the additional advantages of offering plenty of room for expansion and a cheap and plentiful labour force in Norwich and in the adjoining hamlets of Old Lakenham and Trowse. The move from Stoke began in 1854 and was staggered over the next eight years, the whole process being closely supervised by Jeremiah James who showed his flair for organization and control.

One of the reasons given by Colmans for transferring production from Stoke was to relieve local inhabitants from the noise of the stampers used to crush mustard seed. The unfortunate citizens of Norwich were soon to experience an even worse nuisance as a result of the firm's transfer to Carrow. In 1852 Colmans were summoned before local magistrates to answer the charge that they were carrying on 'a new and offensive manufacture' in making cattle cake from the fibres left over after the production of starch. A local schoolmaster complained that the smell from this process would drive his pupils away, a man who hired out boats on the river feared the loss of all his customers and a lady living nearby complained of nausea and lack of appetite. In its defence the firm summoned as witnesses, first, workers in the starch department who claimed that far from being impaired their appetites had actually improved, and then a Norwich cloth dyer who said the offending odour would destroy the malaria, typhus and cholera germs which were prevalent in the low-lying marshy area. The firm was fined £50 with £9 costs but the conviction was later overturned on appeal. Local disquiet was allayed when Jeremiah James bought up the land around his new works. It turned out to be a very useful purchase as it enabled the firm to expand on the Carrow site as business increased.

Mustard making was the first major manufacturing operation to move from Stoke Cross to Carrow. A mustard mill and packing department were opened in 1856, the same year that the counting-house staff were installed at the new site. Most of the mustard seed was bought at Wisbech, Cambridgeshire, from farmers in the Fenlands, although the firm also obtained supplies from Yorkshire, Essex and the Netherlands. It was brought direct to the new mill either by railway or by boat. After being dressed and dried in kilns, the seed was passed through rollers to remove the outer husk and the resultant mixture of husk and kernel was then pulverized by giant mechanical pestles and mortars known as stampers. The flour thus produced was sieved to remove the husks and other impurities. Finally the different varieties of brown and white mustard flour, which had been milled separately, were blended to make the powder which was sold to the public.

Mustard had long been known both for its medicinal properties and as a condiment. Before the days of refrigeration, it was valued for its preservative properties and for its strong flavour which helped to disguise the taste of meat which could no longer be considered entirely fresh. Until the early eighteenth century mustard seeds had been brought to table and crushed with a pestle and mortar or the handle of a knife. Then in 1720 a Mrs Clements of Durham had the idea of grinding and sifting the seeds to produce a fine powder. A mustard factory was estab-lished twenty-two years later in London by Messrs Keen but the product tended to be regarded as something of a luxury item. The great achievement of Jeremiah James Colman was to create a mass demand for an easily prepared high-quality mustard and to associate it firmly in the mind of consumers with the name of his firm so that anyone going into a shop was as likely to ask for a packet of Colmans as for a packet of mustard. Like George Palmer, he was helped by the great growth in spending power and the rise of the retail grocery trade in Britain in the second half of the nineteenth century. But much of Colman's success can be directly attributed to his appreciation of the importance of marketing and publicity and of the key role that packaging could play in promoting the sale of his products.

Most of the mustard powder produced at Stoke Cross had left the works in large wooden casks weighing between 9 and 144 pounds. It went directly in this form to grocers who would weigh out the quantity required by customers and put it in a paper bag. The company had experimented a little with packing mustard in plain cylindrical tins and in bottles for its export trade but there was no decoration on these containers. It was not until the move to Carrow that Colmans started individual packaging and intro-duced the bright yellow labels and highly decorated containers that have been so distinctive a feature of its products ever since.

Jeremiah James himself seems to have been the force behind this innovation. A seven-storey tin workshop was opened at Carrow at the same time as the mustard mill. By the late 1880s twenty-five different sizes of container were being made there, each aimed for a different market. They ranged from the halfpenny tinfoil bag and the famous penny oval tin to highly decorated one-pound octagonal canisters and special pictorial tins for the Christmas trade which contained five or six pounds of mustard. The standard upright rectangular tins with rounded edges still in use today were introduced in the 1870s. In an adjoining packing department boys and girls filled the tins from large bins of mustard powder and labelled them. Another group filled jars and bottles for the export market. As soon as each container was filled, its lid was fastened down and securely sealed with an impress of the bull's head trade mark.

This trade mark, which after a brief absence in the 1960s once again adorns every Colmans product, played an important part in establishing the name and reputation of the firm. It was almost certainly introduced in 1855 and was one of the first to be registered under the Trade Marks Act of 1875. There are various theories as to why Colman should have chosen a bull's head. Some say it was as a symbol of strength, others to reinforce the message that mustard is the perfect complement to beef. But whatever the reason, it has served the firm well. The bull's head came to be a symbol of excellence. Like other manufacturers, Colmans added wheatflour to its cheaper grades of mustard, but its top grade was uniquely free from any additives or impurities. The firm received a significant boost from the Sale of Food and Drugs Act of 1875 which required foodstuffs to be described as 'mixed' if they were adulterated in any way. Unlike its competitors, Colmans could use the phrase 'Warranted Pure' on the labels of its top grade mustards. It could also display the Royal Coat of Arms and warrants of appointment from several of the crowned heads of Europe. In 1866 a special warrant was granted by Queen Victoria and the following year by Napoleon III of France. The Prince of Wales followed suit in 1868 and Victor Emmanuel II of Italy in 1869. In 1878 Jeremiah Colman was decorated with the French Cross of the Legion of Honour as a personal award for the excellence of his products displayed at the Paris Exhibition of that year. The various medals won in international exhibitions, among them London, Dublin, Moscow, Vienna and Melbourne, were also illustrated on the yellow labels of the mustard tins, another feature which has continued to the present day.

Jeremiah James was not content to let his distinctive packaging with its bold red lettering sell his mustard unaided. He also embarked on a major advertising campaign. Posters featuring the bull's head trade mark appeared in shops around the country – the earliest surviving one dates from 1869. An advertising department was set up at Carrow in the late 1870s with separate sub-departments to deal with indoor and outdoor displays. Large enamel signs, manufactured at the Carrow works, were erected at prime sites on railway stations and main road junctions. The firm's own railway waggons were painted yellow with a picture of the bull's head and 'Colman's mustard traffic' printed in large red letters on the side. Promotional material like display cards, calendars, diaries, children's books, pencil sharpeners, magnifying glasses, clothes pegs, paper weights and mirrors were distributed in large quantities to spread the name Colman in homes, shops and schools throughout the land. Mustard pots made by Doultons of Lambeth were given to cafés and restaurants. The firm was one of the first in Britain to create a distinctive logo and use it to spectacular effect to establish its brand image and keep its name constantly before the public.

The firm actually had some difficulty in coping with the enormous demand which its skilful packaging and advertising had created. A private note by Jeremiah James in 1872 recorded that there were 1,392 invoices for outstanding orders which had not yet been executed. At one stage he considered producing a French or prepared mustard, but the demand for the ordinary mustard powder, which was sold in a number of different strengths, was so great that there was no incentive to diversify. The company did introduce mustard plasters for medicinal use in 1885, selling them under the name 'sinapism', but otherwise it was quite content to concentrate on the simple powdered condiment and to make its profit, in the words of the well-known adage, from the mustard that people left on their plates.

Although mustard was the mainstay of the Carrow factory, it was not the only product made there. At Stoke, Colmans had been noted for their starch and had indeed won an award at the 1851 exhibition in the Crystal Palace for rice starch, the manufacturing process for which they had patented two years earlier. In 1859 a starch works was opened at Carrow, replacing the temporary structure which had caused offence because of its smell. In the new factory starch was manufactured entirely from rice which was steeped in a solution of caustic soda, ground and the liquor then run into large vats filled with water where the cellulose and gluten sank to the bottom, leaving the starch in suspension. The liquid starch was then transferred to zinc-lined vats, where the water was drawn off and it was left to solidify. After being cut into 6-inch cubes, the solidified starch was next dried in ovens and then scraped by girls to remove the outside crust before being wrapped up in paper and tied with twine. The cubes were then put into ovens again to be baked for several days during which time they became 'crystallized'.

Most of the starch which the firm produced in its early days had been sold in large five-pound blocks to retailers who then cut it up for their customers. As with mustard, the move to Carrow heralded a revolution in packaging. The starch crystals were now often wrapped in decorated cardboard boxes. In 1880 pictorial boxes were introduced decorated with characters from Shakespeare and scenes from the life of British monarchs. The firm produced coloured starches as well as the conventional white variety and it patented a special starch which would make cotton and linen fabrics non-inflammable. This was much in demand among the wearers of wide crinoline dresses which were a potential fire hazard. Although Colmans never achieved the near-monopoly position in starch manufacture that they had in mustard they took a major share in the British market and in 1862 acquired the Bethnal Green Starch Company in order to save transport costs by having a manufacturing and distribution centre in London. Carrow remained the main production centre and by the mid-1880s between 250,000 and 400,000 boxes of starch were being packed there every week and the stock of labels amounted to more than 25 million. The starch-packing department employed hundreds of girls whose hair was filled with dust, giving them the appearance of wearing powdered wigs.

Colmans had always been flour millers and in 1861 this part of the firm's activities was transferred from Stoke. The firm went on making high-quality flour at Carrow for the next hundred years, adding self-raising flour to its range in 1892. Once again, packaging was all-important to its success. Colmans were among the first millers to bag their own flour individually rather than dispatch it in large sacks to be sold by bakers and grocers. That way they made more profit on each pound sold and at the same time advertised and established a brand image among customers. In 1864 production of cornflour started at Carrow. Despite its name it was made out of rice and sold in packets which carried testimonials from several eminent doctors and a lengthy recommendation from the *Lancet* as to its usefulness 'in the hospital and sick-room'.

The fourth main product manufactured at Carrow was laundry blue, used for enhancing the whiteness of clothes after washing. A blue mill was established there in 1862. Initially the product was made from raw indigo which was mixed with other ingredients and then pressed into 'thumbs' by girls, but in 1872 the company largely switched to using ultramarine which was pressed into moulds in the shape of cubes, oblongs and balls. These were then wrapped in mauve paper and sold as 'Azure Blue' in one-pound, half-a-pound and quarter-pound packs which bore the impressive legend, 'as used in the Royal Laundry'. In the 1872 Moscow International Exhibition Colmans won a gold medal for their azure and indigo blues. Their mustard and starch won the only grand gold medals awarded and its cornflour the only grand silver medal, which was the highest award in the exhibition. The Norwich firm now had a fully international reputation.

True to the Nonconformist principles of thrift and good husbandry, Jeremiah James was determined to make maximum use of the by-products of the main manufacturing processes at Carrrow. The rice fibre and gluten left over from starch production were pressed into square cakes and sold as cattle food advertised as containing 'excellent flesh and muscle-forming properties'. The husks of the mustard seed were crushed to extract oil and then made into a corrugated cake which was sold to farmers as manure and was apparently much sought after in France as a fertilizer for vineyards. The oil expressed from the husks was refined and used as a lubricant. It was also sold for the relief of rheumatism.

This principle of 'waste not, want not' permeated the entire

Carrow works and seems to have affected the workers as much as the proprietor. The drill bags in which mustard seed from the Netherlands was packed were converted into 'beautiful summer suits'. The sawdust and shavings from the cooperage where casks and boxes were made were put into sacks and taken to Great Yarmouth where they were used for the curing of herring. Discarded grain husks from the flour mills and rice fibre from the starch factory were used to feed a herd of pigs which were slaughtered at Christmas time, the hams being smoked and used for sandwiches at the annual staff tea and the other parts being cut and distributed to the workforce in joints appropriate to the size of their families.

Carrow became an almost completely self-sufficient industrial community. Jeremiah James was determined that everything that the company needed should be made on site. In addition to the mills, manufacturing and packaging departments, tinshop and cooperage, there was a factory for making cardboard boxes, a printing shop for labels and stationery and a paper mill which used waste materials such as fibre, rice bags and rags to produce wrappers and packaging material. The works had its own foundry, smithy and engineering department complete with a store containing supplies of iron, steel, lead, glue, twine, paint and everything else that might conceivably be needed. A sawmill supplied the carpenters and coopers with timber and also provided coffins for employees – a practice that continued until 1949. Managers and office staff were laid to rest in well-matured 'staff oak' and given brass nameplates while workers had to make do with coffins of 'hedgerow oak' and black nameplates. There was an extensive system of railway sidings and a riverside complex of wharves and warehouses. Carrow had its own fleet of barges, its own fire brigade and its own post and telegraph office with direct private lines to the London office. It even had its own water supply provided from an artesian well which had been sunk in 1859 and which produced 12,000 gallons a minute.

By the 1880s 2,200 people were employed at Carrow to keep all these operations going, while a further 4,000 directly depended on the works for their livelihood. Over this vast workforce Jeremiah

James directly presided as a somewhat autocratic but essentially benevolent patriarch. From the time of his marriage to Caroline Cozens-Hardy, the daughter of a north Norfolk landowner, in 1856, he lived in a plain eighteenth-century house which stood on the edge of the Carrow works. From the windows of Carrow House, which the Colmans occupied for forty years, he could look out on the 26 acres of mills, granaries, warehouses, factories and workshops which he had created. It was hardly surprising that one of his favourite sayings came to be 'we don't use the word "can't" at Carrow'.

From the beginnings of the firm the Colmans had taken a strong interest in the welfare and needs of their employees. At Stoke Cross they had set up a benefit society to provide support for the sick and elderly, a school, a reading club and a library and the singing classes in which Jeremiah James had taken a prominent part as a young boy. His mother had also set up and run a clothing club. He continued this philanthropic tradition at Carrow. To encourage habits of thrift, he established provident funds, clothing funds and compulsory accident insurance and every employee who was not insured against sickness through a friendly society was compelled to join a works scheme. In 1857 he moved the school to rooms near the new works and wrote to all employees telling them that it was available for their children. 'Feeling that as employers we are bound to aid you in the education of your children', he wrote, 'my Partners and myself will remunerate the teachers.' Nominal fees of one penny per week for the first child in a family and a halfpenny for subsequent children were charged to provide money for prizes. In his letter Colman went on to lay down the curriculum which was to include reading, writing, spelling, arithmetic, grammar, geography, history, drawing and 'also the diligent and careful teaching of the Sacred Scriptures'. Liberally minded Nonconformist that he was, he added, 'As regards religious subjects, the Bible and the Bible alone will be taught, nothing that bears the stamp of sect, party or denomination will intrude'.

The school started with twenty-three children. It soon outgrew its original premises and in 1864 moved to new purpose-built premises on Carrow Hill overlooking the works. By 1870 it was providing education for 333 pupils and this before the days of compulsory primary schooling. There was a strong stress on teaching practical and manual skills. At the instigation of Caroline Colman woodwork, domestic economy and Venetian ironwork were introduced into the curriculum while Jeremiah's influence was responsible for the inclusion of gardening and bee keeping. The school became something of a model establishment and was visited by Matthew Arnold and other leading Victorian educationists. The firm went on bearing its entire cost until 1891 when a government grant was applied for and attendance at the school, which by now had 637 pupils, was made completely free. In 1900 management was handed over to the local school board. The building, still clearly visible on Carrow Hill, now houses a second-hand furniture store.

Shortly before their marriage Jeremiah James had written to Caroline: 'I hope we shan't lead an ideal selfish existence, for I am sure that it won't be a happy one if we do. Influence, position and wealth are not given for nothing, and we must try and use them as we would wish at the last we had done.' Caroline was, in fact, to be the moving spirit behind many of the pioneering welfare schemes introduced at the Carrow works. Like her husband, she was deeply religious and serious minded. A devout Methodist, she was contributing articles to the *Wesleyan Times* at the age of seventeen. She personally supervised and played the harmonium at the Sunday School which was held in the Carrow School and catered for 570 children by the 1890s.

One of the most important ventures which Caroline Colman launched at Carrow was the works kitchen which was started in 1868. This supplied workers with cheap food and drink – a quarter pound of hot meat with gravy and potatoes cost threepence and a pint of coffee and milk a penny. The prices covered the bare cost of raw materials with the costs of preparation and cooking being met by the company. Caroline acted as 'lady superintendent' of the kitchens and specified that they should open at 5.45 in the morning for early tea and coffee for those who had a long walk into work.

In 1872 a self-help medical club and dispensary was set up providing free medical attention for employees' wives and children in return for a payment of a penny a week. At the same time a sick visitor was appointed to work among the male employees and investigate cases of special need. Two years later he was joined by a welfare officer who visited the homes of the female workers and organized sewing classes in their dinner hour. Mrs Colman told her that her job was 'to teach them to be better women and better wives as they grow up'. In 1878 the firm appointed what is generally agreed to have been the first industrial nurse in Britain. Philippa Flowerday was engaged by Caroline Colman to work in the dispensary in the mornings and then visit the sick in their homes, taking with her a large bag of food from the works kitchen.

There was a strongly paternalist quality about the welfare schemes introduced at Carrow. Concerned about the loneliness of the girl employees, and 'the moral danger surrounding them', Caroline established a residential home with a matron in charge. On her instructions, every worker was given an annual almanack at Christmas with an appropriate religious text for each day of the succeeding year 'and some practical hints and receipts relating to food and hygiene'. She also supervised an annual distribution of parcels and blankets to needy families. This took place every October in the works kitchen and the opportunity for moralizing was not lost. Caroline's daughter later recalled that 'the women came up to tea and to receive their parcels from my mother, together with some word of encouragement or, if necessary, exhortation'.

Annual tea parties were laid on at the works on Whit Tuesday. Admission tickets to these events were of two kinds, one allowing the holders to partake of beer and the other for teetotallers who preferred ginger beer. The meal consisted of ham sandwiches and plum cake with nuts and fruit to follow. One worker made himself a special capacious jacket out of seed bags in which he could store a collection of nuts to take home. By 1877 the number of people attending the tea parties had become too big for comfort – more than 5,000 sat down that year – and they were abandoned in favour of an all-day paid holiday. There was another day off for the office staff in September following the annual mustard delivery in which a train hauling 170 or more waggons laden with tins for the Christmas trade left Trowse station. Virtually all the office staff were engaged in loading these trains and they were rewarded by a cruise on the river on chartered steamers.

Unlike some other philanthropically minded employers, Jeremiah James Colman did not build a model village for his workforce. He did, however, build a large number of houses for them in the villages of Lakenham and Trowse. Himself a keen gardener, winning a prize at the Crystal Palace Tulip Show in 1856, he believed that every man should have his own plot of land on which to grow vegetables and flowers, and he provided the land for more than 200 allotments which were let out at an annual rental of ninepence a rod to Carrow workers.

His philanthropic interests were not confined to his own workforce. He was one of the leading figures in the charitable, religious and public life of East Anglia in the second half of the nineteenth century and was also of some importance on the national political stage. That he found time for so many outside activities was a tribute to his superb powers of delegation. A team of carefully chosen departmental managers kept the Carrow works running smoothly and efficiently on a day-to-day basis and allowed the proprietor the time to devote himself to an extraordinary range of outside interests.

Religion was the dominating motive and force in Jeremiah James Colman's life. Brought up a Baptist, he became a Congregationalist in the 1870s but was never a narrow sectarian and, although a staunch Nonconformist, was not unfriendly to the Established Church. Like Samuel Morley, he was much involved in the celebrations in 1862 to mark the bicentenary of the birth of English Nonconformity and was also a keen supporter of the Salvation Army, the YMCA (from 1860 until his death he was president of the Norwich branch) and the Pleasant Sunday Afternoon Movement which aimed to provide innocent and improving activities for working men on their one day off during the week. He was also an enthusiast for Christian missionary work overseas, and when he and Caroline moved into Carrow House he chose a dining table 16 feet long so they could hold missionary breakfast parties.

Education was another major interest. He was particularly keen on extending technical education, a field in which he felt

Britain lagged dangerously far behind the rest of Europe. He helped to establish a technical school in Norwich and was actively involved in adult education and the night school movement. Like so many of his background and experience, he believed strongly in the educative value of inculcating the principles of self-help, mutual aid and thrift and keenly supported the establishment of friendly societies and savings banks. Although not himself a teetotaller, he was a strong friend of the temperance movement and believed that drink stood at the root of many contemporary social ills. He succeeded in closing six of the nine public houses within a quarter-mile radius of Carrow by buying out the landlords. He erected a coffee house at Trowse as a counter-attraction and provided facilities at his works for the dispensing of non-alcoholic drinks.

It was partly through his interest in promoting education and religious equality that Jeremiah James was led first into local and then into national politics. He was first elected to Norwich Town Council in 1859 at the age of twenty-nine and remained until 1871 when he was elected MP for the City, a position which he was to occupy for the next twenty-four years. He was successively sheriff and mayor of Norwich, a magistrate and justice of the peace and deputy-lieutenant of the county of Norfolk. He also wielded much influence locally through the *Eastern Daily Press* which he was instrumental in launching in 1870 as a Liberal newspaper for East Anglia. The paper is still going strong today and his great grandson, Timothy, is the present chairman of the Eastern Counties Newspapers group which publishes it.

In many ways Jeremiah James was a reluctant politician. He hated the show and ostentation of political life. When after one election victory a crowd of supporters insisted on uncoupling the horses from his carriage and themselves dragging it in triumph through Norwich, he quietly got out and walked home, leaving the coachman to enjoy the procession. Within Parliament he was not a frequent speaker, believing that 'one of the great virtues of a member of that assembly is to be able to hold his tongue and I am sure that giving a good and right vote is quite as useful as quoting poetry to the House of Commons'. But there was no doubt of his

94

commitment to the Liberal cause, which was total and absolute. He entered the House of Commons, where he was introduced by Samuel Morley, when Gladstone's first great ministry was in full swing, and fully supported its measures to bring religious equality to Nonconformists, extend democracy through the secret ballot, tighten up the drinking laws and reform the Civil Service. He was a fervent believer in the Gladstonian creed of peace, retrenchment and reform and a passionate adherent to the gospel of free trade.

There was, however, one matter on which he was to prove something of a thorn in his leader's side. When in 1890 Charles Stewart Parnell, the leader of the Irish Nationalists, was cited as co-respondent in a divorce case and tacitly admitted his adultery, the Nonconformist world was outraged and demanded his resignation. Colman wrote to Gladstone warning him of the alienation of Nonconformist electors if Parnell was allowed to stay on, and in a letter to another leading politician he named five seats in East Anglia which the Liberals would lose at the next election unless their adulterous ally was removed. Gladstone knew that Parnell's leadership of the Irish Nationalists and his alliance with the Liberals offered the only real hope of solving the Irish problem, but he was forced by the pressure of Colman and others to submit to the strict and puritanical demands of what one correspondent to *The Times* christened 'the Nonconformist Conscience'.

The severity with which Jeremiah James regarded adultery in high places was but one aspect of a strong vein of puritanism which ran through his character. Apart from cricket, which he enjoyed, he generally shunned recreations and social gatherings. He once opened a bazaar and vowed that he would never do so again because he felt it was a time-wasting event, and he also refused to lay foundation stones, commenting 'I could not with sufficient dignity declare the stone well and truly laid'. He despised the race for riches which he saw animating many of the merchants and tradesmen of Britain and strongly disapproved of the granting of titles. When Gladstone asked leave to submit his name to the queen for a baronetcy in 1893 he politely but firmly declined. In all things he preferred simplicity and directness to fuss and pretentiousness. He once said of a fellow Liberal candidate, 'Tell him to use less Latin and more words easily understood by ordinary men'.

The same utter honesty and straightforwardness characterized his business dealings. He believed that his position as head of a great manufacturing enterprise carried with it profound responsibilities and duties. He took a generally enlightened view on labour questions, supporting the principle that employers should be liable for accidents and injuries suffered at work and welcoming the advent of trade unionism. Like Samuel Morley, however, he had some misgivings towards the end of his life about the rise of full-time trade union negotiators and the increasing polarization of capital and labour. He clung optimistically to the view that 'all differences of opinion between employer and employed might, if both had a determination to do what was right, be amicably settled'. He himself tried to keep close to his men. At the end of a long day when a party of 500 workers from Carrow had visited the 1862 International Exhibition in London he noted 'I am especially glad that I made up my mind to go with the men in the same train'.

Towards the end of his life he spent less time at Carrow and more at the seaside home which he and Caroline had bought at Corton, on the coast 1½ miles north of Lowestoft. There he entertained a number of Nonconformist ministers and Liberal politicians, including on two occasions Mr and Mrs Gladstone. He also busied himself building houses, a coffee parlour, a village hall and a school for the local inhabitants. Although now in his sixties, he still sometimes rose at four in the morning to tend the rose gardens and put in two hours' work before family prayers and breakfast. He often continued working until 7.30 in the evening and then devoted the later part of the evening to going through the firm's accounts. Carrow still remained very much at the centre of his interests and, despite his habit of delegation, there was no doubt in anyone's mind there about the ultimate source of authority. As a visitor to the works in the late 1890s put it,

The two thousand and some hundreds of workers may, not in-aptly, be compared to a well-equipped industrial army, divided into its regiments, companies, sub-divisions and sections, each with its appointed officers, receiving orders from the general's quarters, and carrying them into effect with despatch and fidelity. Throughout the works may be noticed a feeling of pride in the monuments of peaceful victories.

It is easy to paint an over-idyllic picture of life at Carrow. A high proportion of the workforce were women and children, particularly in the packaging department where wages were low and the atmos-phere often dusty and crowded. As in most other factories of the time, boys were laid off once they reached the age of sixteen or eighteen and girls when they got married. In 1895 the *Eastern Weekly Leader*, a radical local paper, carried a series of articles from an ex-employee at Colmans who claimed that he and others had been fired from the company for complaining of sweated labour in the starch department. He complained that there were no fixed hours, lateness and laughter were punished by workers being sent home and losing a day's wages, and girls had to stand scraping and packing starch from seven in the morning until five in the evening for wages of only five to eight shillings a week. Such comments are rare, however, and on the whole the workers at Carrow seem to have felt themselves well treated. A carpenter who served Jeremiah James for fifty years at Stoke Mill, Carrow and Corton, spoke for many when he said, 'I have always found that he very much appreciated any man who tried to do his duty to the best of his ability, and to such of his employees he was always most kind, thoughtful and generous'.

In the last few years of his life Jeremiah James was much affected by the loss of his wife and his son, Alan, in whose memory he bought a site for a new children's hospital in Norwich and established a children's playground. He still continued to take an active interest in affairs at Carrow and in 1896 he converted the firm into a limited liability company with a capital of £1,350,000, taking care to insert into the memorandum of association a clause committing the direc-tors to support certain charitable institutions. One of his last public

appearances was in London at the end of May 1898 at the funeral of
W. E. Gladstone. In September his mother died at the age of 93
after just one day's illness. Three days later he himself was dead.
His funeral brought Norwich to a standstill. Behind his coffin the
firm's best horses drew a column of waggons laden high with
wreaths and tributes and 1,200 of the 3,000-strong workforce
followed on foot while the rest lined the streets. Shops throughout
the city were closed as Norwich mourned the man who had helped
to turn it from a somewhat corrupt borough with a declining
woollen industry into a citadel of reform and a thriving manufacturing centre.

With his death there was an inevitable change in the character
of the firm over which he had presided for 44 years. From now on
there was to be a less paternalistic and patriarchal atmosphere.
But he had taken care to ensure that the strong commitment to the
welfare of the workforce which had always distinguished Colmans
would continue beyond his death by providing in his will a sum of
£2,000 for twenty years to be used to help employees, ex-
employees, widows and any others in need. In 1900 the directors
established an old age pension scheme at Carrow in his memory.

The twentieth century has seen Colmans merge with two other
old-established companies to become one of the leading food and
household products manufacturers in Britain. In 1903 the firm
amalgamated with Keen, Robinson & Company, who had begun
mustard production in 1724 and were also manufacturers of the
two leading infant and invalid foods in Britain, patent barley and
patent groats. Nine years later Colmans acquired Joseph Farrow
& Company, the only other remaining mustard makers of any size
in the country. In 1938 a merger took place with Reckitt & Company, the other major manufacturers of washing blue and starch.
Sir James Reckitt, a Quaker who had built up the starch works
first established by his father, Isaac, in Hull in 1840, was a near
contemporary of Jeremiah James Colman and a man very much in
the same mould.

Colmans of Norwich is now a major division of Reckitt & Colman
plc. The firm has retained its link with the Colman family – Sir
Michael Colman, a descendant of the London branch of the family,

is chairman of the board of directors and Jeremiah James's great-grandson, Timothy, is a non-executive director. It has also remained at Carrow. The factory buildings are clearly visible to those travelling to Norwich by train. They are dominated by a huge silo, the top of which resembles the upper deck of a battleship, complete with aerials and what look like two squat funnels. About 1,300 people work at Carrow today making Robinson's baby foods, soft drinks and barley water, Gale's honey and OK sauces as well as powdered and prepared mustard, condiments and sauces. Mustard tins are still made in the original tinshop and Carrow House now houses offices. In 1973, as part of the celebrations to mark the 150th anniversary of the founding of the firm, the Mustard Shop was opened in Bridewell Alley in the centre of Norwich. Here visitors can buy speciality mustards and inspect an interesting display on the history of the company. They can also pay homage to the man who convinced the British public that no meal was complete without a little mustard on the side of the plate.

6
ANDREW CARNEGIE
(1835–1919)

Andrew Carnegie's life story has all the ingredients of a classic rags to riches romance. In common with millions of others, his family was forced by economic hardship to emigrate from Britain to the United States and he began his working life at the age of thirteen earning $1.40 a week as a bobbin boy in a cotton factory in Pittsburgh, Pennsylvania. Twenty years later he contemplated retiring on the $50,000 annual income that he was earning from his investments. But he went on to build up the largest iron and steel works in the United States, and when he finally sold his business in 1901 it was for $480 million, making him easily the richest man in the world. He devoted the last two decades of his life to being 'a distributor of wealth for the benefit of mankind'. In all, he gave away well in excess of $350 million, most of it to trusts which he set up on both sides of the Atlantic.

Carnegie's approach to philanthropy differed markedly from that of the five entrepreneurs whom we have already looked at. So far what we have seen has basically been the exercise of straightforward Christian charity by rich men with consciences who gave away their money to good causes. Carnegie disliked the whole idea of charity. He was totally opposed to any kind of philanthropy which encouraged notions of clientship and dependence among its recipients. His principle in giving was rather to encourage self-help. As he put it, 'The main consideration should be to help those who will help themselves, to provide part of the means by which those who desire to improve may do so; to give those who desire to rise the aids by which they may rise, but rarely or never to do all'. This principle found expression in the creation of more than 2,500 public libraries and in substantial grants to education and research.

Carnegie adopted a philosophical approach to his philanthropy, working out his ideas in an article entitled 'The Gospel of Wealth'. Believing that 'the man who dies rich dies disgraced', he himself found that it was impossible to spend all his money in his own lifetime. The solution which he hit upon was to establish grant-making trusts with broad and flexible terms of reference that would continue to distribute the income from his endowments long after his death. As we shall see, Joseph Rowntree adopted the same approach and it was also used to distribute the wealth accumulated by George Cadbury and William Hesketh Lever.

Unlike most of the other industrialists in this book, Carnegie was not a model employer. He paid low wages in an effort to cut costs to the minimum and, perhaps because of his desire to avoid paternalism and charity, he did not establish model housing or other welfare facilities for his workers, although when he was rich he did provide them with pensions and handsome compensation for accidents. But his public beneficence was on a scale which few individuals have come near to equalling and his continuing impact on the world today, through the agency of the eleven trusts which he created in the United States and the United Kingdom, is considerable.

Andrew Carnegie was nicknamed the Star-Spangled Scotch-man. Although he spent most of his adult life and made all of his fortune in the United States, he returned as often as he could to his native Scotland and was fiercely proud of his homeland. In what was a remarkably accurate description of his own character, he wrote:

It's a God's mercy I was born a Scotchman, for I do not see how I could ever have been contented to be anything else. The little plucky dour deevil, set in her own ways and getting them too, level-headed and shrewd, with an eye to the main chance always and yet so lovingly weak, so fond, so led away by song or story, so easily touched to fine issues, so leal, so true! Ah! you suit me, Scotia, and proud I am that I am your son.

His romantic patriotism may well have derived at least in part from the fact that his birthplace, Dunfermline, a few miles north of the Firth of Forth, was the ancient seat of the kings of Scotland. It was in the attic of a tiny weaver's cottage that he first saw the light of day in 1835. The room, which can still be seen today, served as bedroom, sitting room, dining room and play room for the Carnegie family. Andrew's father, William, earned a 'poor but honest' living weaving damask cloth for table linen on a hand-operated loom. His mother, Margaret, was the daughter of a shoemaker. Both parents shared a love of Scottish folk song and young Andrew received a solid grounding in the traditions and history of Scotland from his uncle, George Lauder, who delighted in telling him about heroic figures in the nation's past. Two in particular impressed the young boy by their courage and wisdom, Robert the Bruce, the great patriot who was buried in Dunfermline Abbey, and Robert Burns, who was indirectly responsible for Andrew's first earnings, a penny awarded by his schoolmaster for his excellent recitation of the poem 'Man was made to mourn'. In later life he often asked himself when faced with a difficult situation what Bruce or Burns would have done in similar circumstances and he kept constantly in mind Bruce's famous aphorism: 'If at first you don't succeed, try, try, try again' and Burns's injunction 'Thine own reproach alone do fear'.

Andrew was also schooled by members of his family in the principles of radical and democratic politics. His father and his mother's brother had been among the founders of the Political Union set up in Dunfermline in 1831 to agitate for parliamentary reform and an extension of the vote to working men. Bitterly disappointed by the limited provisions of the Great Reform Act of 1832, they went on to become active in the Chartist movement which campaigned for universal manhood suffrage and other political reforms. As a boy Andrew was not allowed to play in Pittencrieff Park, which included the ruins of the old royal palace, because its owner disapproved of the family's radical politics. He wrote later in his autobiography, 'It is not to be wondered at that, nursed amid such surroundings, I developed into a violent young Republican whose motto was "death to privilege"!'

Although it was a less important influence than politics, religion also had an impact on the young boy. His father rejected the harsh doctrines of Calvinism and left the local Presbyterian church when the minister preached on the theme of infant damnation. But William Carnegie remained a devout believer – Andrew recalled him kneeling down every evening to pray – and later found his spiritual home in the Swedenborgian sect. Andrew himself eschewed any particular denomination in favour of a universalist faith which drew on the teachings of several world religions. But he learned several important lessons from the Protestant Christianity in which he was brought up. One of them was to be of considerable use in his later life. It is said that when on his first day at school he was asked to quote a passage from the Bible, he confidently recited the injunction 'Take care of your pence and the pounds will take care of themselves'.

If he showed early in life a sense of the importance of careful management of money, he was also quick to demonstrate the talent for organization and delegation which was to contribute so much to his later success in business. He managed to persuade friends to gather food for his pet rabbits every Saturday in return for the promise that any babies would be named after them. 'My conscience reproves me today', he wrote much later, looking back on this arrangement, 'when I think of the hard bargain I drove with my young playmates, many of whom were content to gather dandelions and clover for a whole season with me, conditional upon this unique reward – the poorest return ever made to labour. Alas! what else had I to offer them! Not a penny.'

While Andrew was striking his first commercial bargains, his father was finding it increasingly difficult to make a living. The introduction of steam machinery was transforming weaving from a cottage to a factory-based industry and displacing the thousands like him who owned or rented hand looms and worked from home. Carnegie remembered clearly the day his father told him that he had no more work and the family conference which followed when his mother suggested that they emigrate to the United States and settle in Pittsburgh where she already had relatives. He recalled also the optimism with which the move across the Atlantic was contemplated, with his mother saying 'It's best for the boys to begin life in a new country' and his father repeating often the words of the song 'To the West, to the West, to the land of the free'. The furniture and the looms were sold and, with £20 borrowed from friends to pay for their passage, the family set off for Glasgow in May 1848 to embark on the voyage that was to take them to the New World. Andrew was just twelve and his brother Tom only five.

The decade in which the Carnegies emigrated from Britain saw more than 2,750,000 people leave to seek a better life abroad, nearly 2 million of them going to the United States. A high proportion came from Ireland, Scotland and Wales which had been particularly hard hit by the poor harvests and potato blight that made for the 'hungry forties'. It was a bold and risky undertaking. The voyage across the Atlantic was still fraught with danger, and job prospects in America were by no means as rosy as they seemed from the other side. The Carnegies were lucky at least in the first respect. Their fifty-day passage to New York on the 800-ton ex-whaler, the *Wiscasset*, was smooth and uneventful – Andrew rather enjoyed it, being able to help the undermanned crew with a number of duties for which he was rewarded by being invited 'to participate on Sundays in the one delicacy of the sailors' mess, plum duff'. There then followed a three-week journey via canals, the Great Lakes and river steamers to Allegheny City near Pittsburgh where the family were able to obtain rent-free lodgings in two rooms above a weaver's shop owned by Margaret's sister-in-law. William Carnegie resumed his old trade of weaving table cloths which he then sold from door to door and Margaret spent the evenings binding shoes, with little Tom waxing the thread and threading the needles for her.

These activities brought in little money and it was clear that Andrew would have to go out to work. A relative suggested that he should be kitted out with a basket of knick-knacks and become a pedlar but his mother refused to countenance such a degrading occupation for her son. In fact, Andrew found a job as a bobbin boy in a cotton factory where his father had also been forced to take work. Shortly afterwards he moved to a bobbin-making factory run by a fellow Scots *émigré*, John Hay, where for the meagre wage of $2 a week he looked after a small steam engine and fire boiler in the cellar. One day Hay had to make out some bills and, not being a good writer or mathematician, he asked Andrew to help him. He was impressed by the thirteen-year-old's ability with words and figures and put him on to helping with the firm's accounts, while still expecting him to carry on with manual tasks like dipping the newly made bobbin spools in vats of evil-smelling oil. In an early display of the initiative and keenness to master new skills which he was to show throughout his business life, Andrew went to evening classes to learn double-entry book-keeping.

In 1850 Andrew Carnegie got his first real break. The manager of the Western Union telegraph office in Pittsburgh, who was a friend of his uncle, appointed him as a messenger boy at a salary of $2.50 a week. Andrew immediately showed himself to be a remarkably diligent apprentice. Determined to master the names and addresses of all the firms in the town to which he might be asked to deliver messages, he set about learning them street by street before he went to sleep every night. 'Before long,' he wrote, 'I could shut my eyes and, beginning at the foot of a business street, call off the names of the firms in the proper order along one side to the top of the street, then crossing on the other side go down in regular order to the foot again.' He also rapidly established himself as the leader of the messenger boys. To prevent the quarrels that inevitably arose as to who should deliver the out-of-town messages which attracted a ten cent bonus payment, he suggested the adoption of a pooling arrangement by which equal amounts would be shared out every week and was made treasurer of the scheme.

The messengers' hours of work were long – they started early in the morning and every other day they did not finish until 10 p.m. But Andrew found time to go to the theatre and concerts and form a debating and literary society with friends. He was also a voracious reader and was overjoyed to hear that a new library was being opened in Pittsburgh for the use of 'working boys'. However, there was some doubt about whether this definition included those, like Andrew, in office and commercial employment or whether it simply applied to those in manual work. In his first foray into print, the young messenger wrote a letter to the *Pittsburgh Dispatch* asking that the library be open to all boys. His request was granted and he became one of the library's most regular users.

After about a year with the telegraph company, Carnegie was occasionally given the job of watching over the downstairs office while the manager was out. Here messages were taken from members of the public and those that came from the operating room were assigned to boys for prompt delivery. He made himself expert in Morse code and at the age of sixteen became only the third person in the United States to be able to interpret the dots and dashes by ear without having to read them off tape. In recognition of his encouraging progress and increased responsibilities his salary was raised to $13.50 a month. On the day that he was awarded this increase, Andrew rushed home and told his nine-year-old brother that one day they would go into business together as Carnegie Brothers and buy their parents a carriage. Gradually he was given further responsibilities at work, being allowed to send the occasional telegraph message himself, and in 1852 being sent out to run a small sub-office about twenty miles from Pittsburgh for two weeks while the operator was away. Later that year he became a fully fledged telegraph operator at a salary of $25 a month.

One of the most important customers of the Pittsburgh telegraph office was Thomas Scott, superintendent of the local division of the Pennsylvania Railroad. Impressed by the enthusiasm and competence of the young man who often took his messages, he took on Andrew Carnegie as his clerk and telegraph operator at a monthly salary of $35. The new recruit, who was just eighteen, quickly showed his ability and his considerable self-confidence. On one occasion he took over the running of the entire line in Scott's absence after an accident, and on another, acting entirely on his own initiative and without any reference to his superiors, he dismissed a member of staff responsible for a derailment. A less broad-minded man might well have sacked his young subordinate for such irregular behaviour, but Scott was extremely impressed by the calm and confident way that Carnegie had handled the two crises.

In 1855 William Carnegie died. From now on Andrew devoted

himself to looking after his mother. Wherever he went, she came too and they lived together until her death. In the same year he made his first investment when, at Scott's suggestion, he put $500 of borrowed money into the Adams Express Company. This was to be the first of many investments in the expanding American railroad network which were to provide the basis of Carnegie's first fortune. One of the most successful was his early stake in railway sleeping cars which, according to his autobiography, came about as a result of a chance meeting on a train journey with their inventor, T. T. Woodruff. Woodruff showed Carnegie a model of his new invention and persuaded him to put money into its development. Within three years his initial modest investment was returning an annual dividend of $5,000.

In 1859 Thomas Scott became vice-president of the Pennsylvania Railroad and appointed Carnegie as manager of the Pittsburgh Division. Two years later the American Civil War broke out and Scott was appointed an assistant secretary of war in the Unionist Government with responsibility for all transportation matters. He recruited Carnegie as his assistant with special oversight of military railroads and telegraphs. Carnegie's first job was to repair the line between Washington and Baltimore which had been cut by Confederate forces near Annapolis Junction. After supervising the repairs, he rode back in triumph to Washington on the footplate of the first engine to use the re-opened line. He was subsequently involved in transporting wounded troops from the first Battle of Bull Run. Carnegie found the strains of war work too much for him and at the end of 1861 he suffered a breakdown in health. He went to Scotland to convalesce, taking his mother with him to Dunfermline. It was the first time that they had been back since emigrating thirteen years earlier. He was struck by the smallness of everything in his home town compared with the vastness of the cities, and opportunities, in his adopted country. 'Here was a city of the Lilliputians', he wrote.

Back in the United States he continued to invest widely in railroad projects, oil wells, telegraph companies and iron works. By 1863 he had an annual income of well over $40,000 of which only $2,400 came from his salary with the Pennsylvania Railroad.

Andrew Carnegie was now on the verge of his most productive period as an entrepreneur. Although he would have been reluctant to admit it as a man of peace, it was war which brought him his greatest opportunity. The long and bitter fight between the Unionist and Confederate armies had shown the vital importance of the railroad network in the United States. It had also shown up the inadequacies of existing technology and materials. The traditional wooden railway bridges were unable to support the weight of fully loaded trains while the shortage of high-quality rails was making large sections of line dangerous for all but very slow-moving convoys.

Carnegie recognized the enormous need that existed for high-quality iron products in the expanding railroad industry and set out to meet it through the establishment of manufacturing companies in and around Pittsburgh. His first venture in 1862 was to help set up a firm to make wrought-iron bridges. First called Piper & Schiffer, it later became the Keystone Bridge Company and was responsible for building the massive structures which carried the lines of the Baltimore and Ohio Railroad across the mighty Ohio River. In 1864 the Superior Rail Mill was built to produce high-quality iron rails and in the same year the Cyclops Iron Company, later the Union Iron Mills, was set up to provide iron for the bridges which were now being built across the United States. Two years later the Pittsburgh Locomotive Works was established to build the engines which were in increasing demand as the railroad network spread westwards in the aftermath of the Civil War.

Although he was just thirty, Andrew Carnegie was now actively involved in the management of four major companies in which he also had a substantial financial stake. He gave up his job in the Pennsylvania Railroad to concentrate on his new role as an entrepreneur. Typically, he determined to master every aspect of the iron and heavy-engineering industries. A holiday in Britain and Europe in 1867 found him not just climbing the Alps and attending concerts in the Crystal Palace but carefully studying the process of washing and coking the dross from Lancashire coal mines. Later that year the expansion of the Pittsburgh businesses forced him to move to New York, the commercial and financial capital of the

United States. Leaving his brother Tom and Henry Phipps, who had been one of the partners involved in setting up the Cyclops Iron Company, to manage the factories, he concentrated on raising further capital, often travelling to Europe to negotiate loans and securities. He was on occasion tempted to abandon his interest in manufacturing altogether and concentrate on finance and banking but he resisted the idea. As he wrote in his autobiography, 'I wished to make something tangible and sell it and I continued to invest my profits in extending the works at Pittsburgh'.

A more serious temptation faced Carnegie in 1868. With total investments of over $400,000 and an annual income of more than $50,000 he felt that the time might have come when he should consider quitting business and devoting himself to more elevating pursuits. In a remarkable memorandum written in a New York hotel he laid down a plan for the future:

> Make no effort to increase fortune, but spend the surplus each year for benevolent purposes. Cast aside business forever, except for others. Settle in Oxford and get a thorough education, making the acquaintance of literary men – this will take three years' active work – pay especial attention to speaking in public. Settle then in London and purchase a controlling interest in some newspaper or live review and give the general management of it attention, taking a part in public matters, especially those concerned with education and improvement of the poorer classes.

Carnegie set himself the target of retiring from business in two years' time when he would be thirty-five. Continuing any longer in the debasing occupation of amassing wealth, which he described in his memorandum as 'one of the worst species of idolatry', would, he felt, degrade his character beyond hope of further recovery. In the event, he was to pursue money making for a further thirty-three years before finally devoting himself to full-time philanthropy at the age of sixty-six. The idea of going to Oxford and getting a thorough education came to naught. The fact was that, as he himself admitted in his memorandum, 'Whatever I engage in

109

I must push inordinately'. In the early 1870s Carnegie was engaged in the challenge of creating a new industry in the world's most dynamic country. It was to take a long time before he could give up that challenge.

The new industry which captured Carnegie's imagination and diverted him from thoughts of retirement was the production of steel. For some time it had been clear to him that, however high its quality, iron was not a sufficiently strong material to cope with the heavy demands made by the relentless expansion of the railroads. On certain sections of the Pennsylvania Railroad the rails were wearing out so fast that they were having to be replaced every six weeks. In 1872 Carnegie went to England to look at the process recently invented by Henry Bessemer which removed impurities from iron to produce a tough and flexible steel. He came back convinced that 'The day of iron is past' and determined to be the man who would initiate the new age of steel in the United States. He already had the largest blast furnace in the world, the Lucy Furnace, built in 1870, named after his sister-in-law and capable of producing 100 tons of pig-iron a day. Now he bought the American rights to Bessemer's process and set about experimenting with turning pig-iron into steel.

In 1874 Carnegie opened his first steel mills, which were named the Edgar Thomson works after the president of the Pennsylvania Railroad who put up much of the capital for the new venture. The main purpose of the factory was to make steel rails for the railroad and it was purposely built on a site at Braddock near Pittsburgh which had access to both the Pennsylvania and Baltimore and Ohio lines as well as to the Ohio River. Within four years its output had surpassed that of every other steel works in the United States.

Carnegie was determined to control the entire steel-making process from the extraction of minerals from the ground to the production of finished steel. He set about buying up the main sources of his raw materials and establishing his own transport network to bring them to Pittsburgh. Soon iron ore mined from the Mesabi Mountains in Minnesota was being carried by Carnegie's ships across the Great Lakes to special docks at Conneaut on Lake Erie; there it was loaded on to waggons for the journey down to

Pittsburgh on the company's own private railway line, the Pittsburgh, Bessemer and Lake Erie railroad. The company had its own coal mines at Connellsville, limestone mines on the east of the Alleghenies and manganese ore mines in Virginia. In 1881 the Edgar Thomson Steel Mills, the Lucy Furnace, the Union Iron Mills and several coal mines and coke ovens were formally brought together in the new company of Carnegie Brothers & Company Limited. Tom Carnegie was chairman of the board and in effect manager of the enterprise, while Andrew concentrated on raising finance for future expansion and on travelling in Europe.

Scotland received increasingly frequent visits from the man who was rapidly becoming one of its richest sons. In 1877 Andrew Carnegie returned to Dunfermline to open a swimming pool for which he had provided the money and to receive the freedom of the burgh, the first of many such honours that he was to receive from towns and cities across the United Kingdom. Four years later he was back with his mother to lay the foundation stone of the first of 660 free libraries that he was to establish in Britain. There was a special significance for Carnegie in establishing a library in his native town. His father had been among a group of five weavers who had formed the first library there by making their own books freely available to any who wished to borrow them. He himself had derived enormous benefit from the library opened for working boys in Pittsburgh. He wrote in his autobiography: 'It was from my own early experience that I decided there was no use to which money could be applied so productive of good to boys and girls who have good within them and ability and ambition to develop it, as the founding of a public library in a community which is willing to support it as a municipal institution.'

Altogether, Andrew Carnegie founded 2,811 free libraries, nearly 2,000 of them in the United States where the first was opened at Braddock in 1889. They perfectly fitted his philosophy of encouraging self-help since only those with a genuine thirst for improvement would enter their portals. He made a rule of providing a building only where the local community would guarantee to stock it with books and foot the running costs. In that way 'all taint of charity is dispelled'. Carnegie did not just intend his libraries to be for bookworms. The building at Braddock also housed a gymnasium, a swimming pool, a boxing ring, a bowling alley and a billiards room. It was later provided with a large adjoining concert hall cum opera house. Listening to music came second only to reading among Carnegie's favourite pastimes and this love was also reflected in his philanthropy. The world-famous Carnegie Hall in New York was opened in 1891 with a concert conducted by Tchaikovsky. Four years later a large library and music hall were opened in Pittsburgh with the promise of a museum and art gallery to follow.

If Carnegie liberally sprinkled Britain and America with free libraries, he positively showered them with church organs. The instrument was a particular favourite of his and in 1873 he presented one to the Swedenborgian church in Allegheny of which his father had been a member. In all he was to give 7,689 organs to churches around the world, 4,059 in the United States, 2,370 in England and Wales and 1,005 in Scotland. He was inundated with requests for many more and devised a complicated questionnaire for applicants to fill in so that he could determine their need and degree of self-reliance.

In 1886 Andrew Carnegie lost both his mother and his brother, Tom, through typhoid fever. The following year, aged 51, he married Louise Whitfield, the daughter of a New York merchant. He had known her for many years and had often ridden with her through Central Park in New York. They honeymooned in the Isle of Wight and then went to Scotland with which she was captivated. When a daughter was born to them in 1897, Louise insisted that they have a summer home in the Highlands. Andrew obliged by buying Skibo Castle on the shores of the Dornoch Firth in Caithness. There he spent every summer, living like a Scottish laird, being woken by a piper every morning as Queen Victoria was at Balmoral, and entertaining leading figures from the literary and political worlds, including Rudyard Kipling and Woodrow Wilson. Another visitor, King Edward VII, was intrigued to see that the flag flying above the castle was made up of the Union Jack and the Stars and Stripes sewn back to back.

Although he was increasingly living the life of a plutocrat, both at his Scottish castle and in his palatial residence in New York, Carnegie did not lose the radical political outlook of his youth. He took a prominent part in Liberal politics when he was in Britain and supported such causes as the abolition of the monarchy and the House of Lords and the disestablishment of the Church of England. In the early 1880s he acquired a chain of newspapers in the Midlands and the North as a vehicle for his views and he made an unsuccessful attempt with a radical MP to turn a well-established paper, the *Echo*, into a journal of republicanism. In 1886 he wrote a book praising the open and democratic constitution of the United States under the title *Triumphant Democracy* and the following year he spoke for an hour and a half in Glasgow on the theme of federalism and commended the principle of Home Rule for Ireland, Scotland and Wales.

There is a marked contrast between Carnegie's advanced and radical political views and his behaviour as an employer. Apart from the provision of libraries and other recreational facilities, his treatment of those who worked for him was not very benevolent. Wages were kept low and conditions of work were bad. Those employed in the furnaces and iron and steel mills worked a twelve-hour day in temperatures which often exceeded 100 degrees Fahrenheit. Saturday was a working day and the only holiday was on Independence Day, the fourth of July. Conditions were particularly tough in the Homestead Steel Mill, the largest open-hearth smelting furnace in the USA, which Carnegie Brothers took over in 1883 largely to make steel beams and girders for skyscrapers. There were said to be few men there over the age of forty. When Sir James Kitson, president of the British Iron and Steel Industry, led a delegation to the United States in 1890 he met one of his old employees who was now working for Carnegie. 'I am quite a different man here', he said, 'from what I was in the old country; I don't know why it is so, whether it is that I live in a stimulating atmosphere, or whether it is the example set me; but I know I have the "go" in me here. I can do more work ... but I also feel and I know that it won't last. I shall be done in ten years.' Another worker at the Homestead plant told an American reporter who was impressed by Carnegie's generosity in providing libraries for his men: 'I have always hoped to educate myself but after working twelve hours how can a man go to the library?'

Between 1875 and 1892 the labour force at the Homestead works was cut by more than a quarter as Carnegie introduced greater mechanization and cut costs to the bone. In that year he proposed to the remaining workers that their wages should be cut and that a company union should take over their negotiating rights from the national union. The workers rejected these proposals and went on strike. While Carnegie was holidaying in Scotland, the chairman of the company, Henry Frick, brought in blackleg labour and hired 300 armed men from the Pinkerton Detective Agency to break up the strike. A bloody battle ensued in which five of the Homestead workers and four of the Pinkerton men were killed, and 300 people were injured. Although Carnegie himself did not publicly condone Frick's brutal suppression of the strike he sent him a private telegram which left little doubt as to his attitude: 'All anxiety gone since you stand firm. Never employ one of these rioters. Let grass grow over the works. Must not fail now.'

In the same month as the Homestead strike Carnegie Brothers bought up further steel mills and became the Carnegie Steel Company Ltd. It was now the largest steel manufacturer in the world with a capital of over $25 million and profits of over $4.5 million. By 1900 the annual profits were up to $40 million, of which $25 million went directly to Carnegie who at last felt that the time had come to put into effect the resolution that he had made thirty-two years earlier and retire from business to devote himself to philanthropy. He had already worked out his ideas on this subject in 'The Gospel of Wealth', an article which first appeared in the *North American Review* in 1889 and which was subsequently re-published in Britain and expanded into a book. Dedicated to the British Liberal statesman, W.E.Gladstone, it laid down a clear moral duty for those who found themselves in Carnegie's position:

The only point required by the gospel of wealth is that the surplus which accrues from time to time in the hands of a man should be administered by him in his own lifetime for that purpose which is seen by him, as trustee, to be best for the good of the people. To leave at death what he cannot take away, and place upon others the burden of the work which it was his duty to perform, is to do nothing worthy. ... The gospel of wealth but echoes Christ's words. It calls upon the millionaire to sell all that he hath and give it in the highest and best form to the poor by administering his estate himself for the good of his fellows, before he is called upon to lie down and rest upon the bosom of Mother Earth.

For all its high moral tone and redistributionist philosophy, there was, in fact, a distinctly élitist and even paternalistic side to Carnegie's gospel. He argued that wealth concentrated in the hands of a few men and properly distributed by them according to the principles of 'scientific philanthropy' was a much more potent force for the general elevation of mankind than it would be if it were generally shared out among everyone. 'The man of wealth', he believed, 'becomes the trustee and agent for his poorer brethren, bringing to their service his superior wisdom, experience, ability to administer, doing for them better than they would or could do for themselves.'

In 1901 Andrew Carnegie finally made the resolution 'to stop accumulating and begin the infinitely more serious task of wise distribution'. He sold the Carnegie Steel Company to J. Pierpont Morgan, the president of the Federal Steel Company, for $480 million, of which is own personal share was $225 million. On the completion of the deal, Morgan congratulated him on being the richest man in the world. Over the next thirteen years Carnegie was to make every effort to divest himself of that title by trying to give away his fortune, but so great was the amount of new interest that accumulated every year that he found it a well-nigh impossible task.

'The Gospel of Wealth' had specified seven particular fields of philanthropy in which the wise trustee of surplus wealth should invest. These were universities, free libraries, hospitals, parks, halls for meetings and concerts, swimming baths and church buildings. In fact, Carnegie himself did not follow this list when it came to choosing projects to endow. Certainly he established

115

many libraries and he also endowed several universities, most notably the Carnegie-Mellon University in Pittsburgh which he founded in 1905 as the Pittsburgh Technical Schools. But hospitals, parks and churches do not figure prominently among his benefactions. Instead he devoted substantial resources to areas of research that were not referred to in the original manifesto.

Carnegie chose to distribute most of his wealth through the creation of endowments and grant-making trusts. The first and most modest of these ventures was the Relief Fund that he established in 1901 to provide pensions for his former employees. In the same year he committed a rather more substantial sum to a trust for the Universities of Scotland, designed to help pay the tutorial fees of poor students and to fund research. The following year the Carnegie Institution of Washington was founded as an independent and non-profit-making research centre operating in the physical and biological sciences. Carnegie's strong interest in teaching led to the foundation in 1905 of the Carnegie Endowment for the Advancement of Learning which began with the specific aim of providing retirement pensions for teachers. Apart from establishing these educational trusts, Carnegie spent more than $15 million on providing buildings and endowing chairs at individual universities and colleges. True to his radical principles, he preferred his money to go to small colleges rather than to the prestigious and already well-endowed institutions of the Ivy League. When Woodrow Wilson, as president of Princeton University, asked Carnegie for a graduate college, a school of law and a school of science, all he got was a lake. This, the donor pointed out, was to take the minds of the students off football, a game which he heartily disliked.

Dunfermline was not forgotten in the great share-out of the wealth of its richest-ever son. In 1902 Carnegie bought Pittencrieff Park, from which he had been excluded as a boy because of his family's radical views. The following year he set up the Carnegie Dunfermline Trust 'to bring into the monotonous lives of the toiling masses of Dunfermline more of sweetness and light'. In addition to an endowment of half a million pounds (later increased to three-quarters of a million), the trustees received the title deeds of the

A Holloway's ointment pot-lid

Thomas Holloway (1800–83)

The Holloway Sanatorium

Sir Titus Salt (1803–76)

Crinoline dresses made of the lustre fabric pioneered by Titus Salt

A view of Saltaire in the 1870s showing the mills, the Congregational chapel, the club and institute and some of the model houses

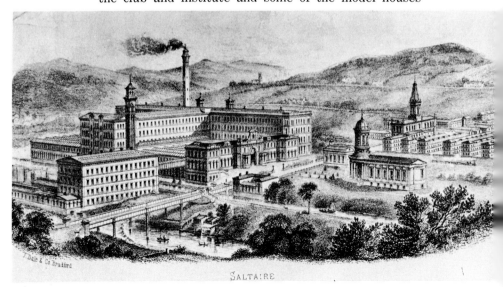

SALTAIRE

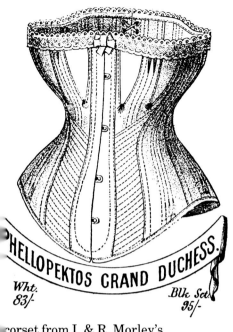

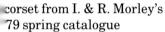

corset from I. & R. Morley's
79 spring catalogue

muel Morley (1809–86) (right),
portrayed in a Spy cartoon of 1872
titled 'Dissent'

e Old Vic Theatre,
1910

One of Huntley & Palmers' early
decorated tins (above)

George Palmer (1818–97)

A biscuit-cutting machine of the kind introduced by Palmer

Jeremiah James Colman (1830–98)

An early Colman's Mustard
advertisement

The Carrow nurse helping an injured employee

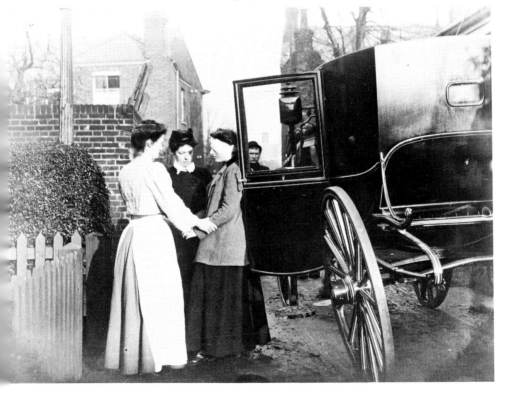

The cooperage department at Colman's Carrow works

Andrew Carnegie (1835–1919)

Carnegie's birthplace
in Dunfermline

An early American skyscraper for
which Carnegie supplied the steel

George Cadbury (1839–1922)

An advertisement stressing the purity of Cadbury's Cocoa Essence, 1893 (right)

Houses in Bournville, built in 1897

Joseph Rowntree (1836–1925)

An advertisement for Rowntree's
Elect Cocoa, *c.* 1910

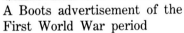

VERMIN POWDER

In times of peace we are all shy of mentioning anything concerning the little parasites that work such havoc when they get on the human body.

In times of War the plague of body vermin is invariably present with those on field service.

Ordinary washing, even with boiling water, will not clear these pests from the clothing or person.

The annoyance and hardship is suffered by both officers and men in the field, preventing sleep and acting injuriously on both the physical and mental being of the men.

Boots *The* Chemists Vermin Powder, scientifically compounded, is successful, convenient, cleanly and absolutely harmless.

Here are just two of its many testimonials :—

A well-known Commanding Officer writes
" *I wish I could get 700 tins a month—they would be a perfect God-send.*"

A Private's practical proof—
" *Will you please send a couple more tins of Boot's Powder? It's great stuff, and has given me a fortnight's respite from one of our enemies out here, and it is just the goods needed. I have appointed myself advertising agent for the product in this regiment*"

Price **9d.** per Box.

Postage 1d. extra.

Girls assembling coronation
tins at Rowntrees in 1911

A Boots advertisement of the
First World War period

Jesse Boot (1850–1931)

Boot's shop at 16–18 Goosegate, Nottingham

William Hesketh Lever (1851–1925)

The controversial way in which Lever used W. P. Frith's painting, 'The New Frock', to advertise Sunlight Soap in 1889

A street scene in Port Sunlight village around the turn of the century

One of the horse-drawn carts used by Lever sales representatives in the 1890s

park and were asked to administer it so that the people of the town could enjoy for ever walking through the grounds of the abbey and the ancient royal palace. He described it as 'the most soul-satisfying gift I ever made'. Among the first projects funded by the Trust were a college of hygiene and physical education and a child welfare system with free medical and dental treatment.

In 1904 Carnegie established a $5 million fund to reward heroes. He had been profoundly moved by the action of a former superintendent of a coal mine near Pittsburgh who, disregarding the fact that he no longer had any connection with the mine, had led a group of rescuers down the pit after an accident had trapped several miners and perished in the attempt to save them. The Carnegie Hero Fund, whose main purpose was to provide pensions for the widows, widowers and children of those who had died in heroic actions, was extended to Britain in 1908 and subsequently to nine other European countries. Carnegie established a pension fund for those who had worked with him in the Pittsburgh Division of the Pennsylvania Railroad and he also maintained a private fund from which he supplied pensions to distinguished friends like Rudyard Kipling and Booker T. Washington, the leading black American of his generation.

Much of Carnegie's money went into projects designed to end wars and bring about world peace. For all his shrewd commercial sense and ruthless industrial practices, he had a strongly idealistic streak, although his declared principles did not always accord with his business practices. In the 1890s he had apparently been happy to preside over a company which made the steel armour plating for the United States battleship fleet. Influenced by the Nonconformist-dominated Peace Society in Britain and by the fervent pacifism of the Quaker politician, John Bright, Carnegie came to believe that if nations and statesmen could be brought to talk to and understand one another, war and conflict would cease. He was a convinced opponent of imperialism and in 1900 attempted to prevent the United States' acquisition of the Philippines. He financed a number of conferences at The Hague to discuss disarmament, and lobbied Kaiser Wilhelm II, President Theodore Roosevelt and Henry Campbell-Bannerman, the British prime minister, on the same subject. Sadly, none of them took the Star-Spangled Scotchman very seriously. Campbell-Bannerman's private secretary dismissed him as 'a funny little manny, wildly keen and enthusiastic, waving his napkin over his head ... full of curious rather elementary and childish internationalist ideas'.

In 1910, on his seventy-fifth birthday, Carnegie announced that he was setting up a $10 million endowment for international peace, 'to hasten the abolition of international war' through conferences, publications and discussion. Although his efforts had little impact on the gathering movement for re-armament in Europe, he achieved more concrete results with the opening of three 'temples of peace' which he paid for, the Pan American Union Building for the Organization of American States in Washington, the Central American Court of Justice in Costa Rica and the International Court of Justice in The Hague. He was also one of the first to advocate the establishment of a League of Nations to arbitrate in cases of disputes between nations and seek to lay down and enforce principles of international law and morality. Less successful was his effort to establish a simplified English language which he hoped would be read and written throughout the world and bring all nations closer together. He set up a Simplified Spelling Board and himself used the abbreviated words which it produced, several of which reflected common American usage like 'catalog' and 'labor', but few others found the system, or the idea, appealing.

By 1910 Andrew Carnegie had given away about $180 million. But he still had almost as much left thanks to the interest constantly accruing on his capital. To use up this remaining portion of his wealth he set up two all-purpose trusts, the Carnegie Corporation of New York (1911) and the Carnegie United Kingdom Trust (1913). The administrators of these funds were given wide discretionary powers to use the money with which they were entrusted in ways that they thought fit to improve the lives of their fellow men. With the establishment of these two funds Carnegie's work as a distributor of wealth was effectively over and he settled down at Skibo to enjoy the last years of his life and to write his autobiography.

His hopes of a happy retirement were, however, to be cruelly shattered by the outbreak of the First World War. The violence and slaughter of the war appalled him and his wife wrote:

Henceforth he was never able to interest himself in private affairs. Many times he made the attempt to continue writing, but found it useless. Until then he had lived the life of a man in middle life – and a young one at that – golfing, fishing, swimming each day, sometimes doing all three in one day. Optimist as he always was and tried to be, even in the face of the failure of his hopes, the world disaster was too much. His heart was broken. A severe attack of influenza followed by two serious attacks of pneumonia precipitated old age upon him.

In the first full month of the war the Carnegies left Scotland for the United States. Andrew was never to return home again. He died in August 1919 at Lennox, Massachusetts, where he had bought a large country mansion, and was buried at the Sleepy Hollow Cemetery in North Tarrytown, New York.

Carnegie's home in New York is now the Cooper–Hewitt Museum and houses the Smithsonian Institute's national museum of design. His birthplace in Dunfermline is now part of a museum devoted to his life and work and Pittencrieff Park remains as he intended it to be, a playground for the town and a fine setting for a statue of its most famous son. Skibo Castle was sold by his daughter, Mrs Margaret Carnegie-Miller, in 1981. The Carnegie Free Library at Braddock, Pennsylvania, is sadly also closed but those in many other towns across both Britain and America are still open, including the original one in Dunfermline which has a bust of Margaret Carnegie in the entrance hall. Between them the seven Carnegie Trusts in the United States and the four in Britain have spent some $2 billion since they were set up and from a current capital of over $1 billion they are still spending over $100 million each year on projects as diverse as the popular children's television series, *Sesame Street*, the Youth Hostels Association and the encouragement of arts among the disabled. Carnegie himself would be delighted to know that they are also busily engaged in restoring the organs in some of Britain's most famous civic halls to their full Victorian glory.

7

GEORGE CADBURY
(1839–1922)

Of the many famous British companies begun by Quakers the best known are almost certainly the chocolate manufacturers, Cadburys of Birmingham and Rowntrees of York. Their products are still household names today and are to be found on the shelves of every supermarket and grocery shop. The two men who built up these firms in the second half of the nineteenth century were among the most enlightened of all Victorian entrepreneurs and shared a commitment to the welfare of their employees which has perhaps never been equalled.

When George Cadbury and Joseph Rowntree entered their respective family businesses in the 1850s chocolate was a luxury product which few people could afford. It was almost exclusively consumed as a drink and was hardly known in the form which we are familiar with today, moulded into bars and sweets for eating. One of the reasons why the manufacture of cocoa and chocolate appealed particularly to Quakers was that it provided a substitute for the demon alcohol. Thanks partly to the efforts of Rowntree and Cadbury, and to the third great Victorian chocolate maker who was also a member of the Society of Friends, Joseph Fry of Bristol, tea, coffee and cocoa came to replace ale as the standard breakfast drinks among the lower and middle classes in Britain and hot drinking chocolate became an increasingly popular alternative to a tot of spirits as a warming and comforting evening beverage. All three men were strong teetotallers and regarded their manufacturing activities as playing an important role in the temperance movement.

Quakerism helped Cadburys, Rowntrees and Frys to prosper in

the confectionery business for the same reason that it assisted the success of Huntley & Palmers, Jacobs and Peek Freans in the biscuit trade. Their insistence on using only pure and unadulterated ingredients revolutionized the British chocolate industry and led directly to the development of the chocolate bars which we happily consume in such vast numbers today. Helped by the reduction in duty on imported cocoa beans and by the general rise in spending power in the middle of the nineteenth century, the trio of Friends transformed chocolate from a luxury to an everyday product and brilliantly exploited the legendary British sweet tooth to create a major industry employing thousands of workers.

The lives of George Cadbury and Joseph Rowntree followed a remarkably similar pattern. Each started out in his father's firm and began chocolate manufacture on a small scale with his brother. Each greatly expanded his business by the application of new technology and the introduction of new products. Each moved his city-centre works to a new site in the country and created a model village for his employees. Both were active in philanthropic and political affairs and had advanced views on social and economic questions. Animating both men was the simplicity, the energy and the overflowing Christian charity of Quakerism at its best.

Strictly speaking, Joseph Rowntree should come before George Cadbury in this book, being the senior by three years. However, it makes more sense to look at Cadbury's life first since he anticipated his great friend and rival by a few years in virtually every important step taken in both the industrial and the philanthropic spheres. Cadbury also died three years before Rowntree and it seems natural to regard him as the senior partner in what was almost a joint venture to transform the economic and social life of Britain.

George Cadbury was born in the Birmingham suburb of Edgbaston in 1839. His father, John, sold tea and coffee at a shop in Bull Street near the city centre and also had a small chocolate factory nearby in Crooked Lane. John Cadbury brought up his six children strictly – he would not allow a piano in the house, although music boxes and the Jew's harp were permitted – and insisted on daily prayers and Bible reading after breakfast. He himself refused to sit in an armchair until he was nearly seventy. George was to develop an equally austere lifestyle, often taking an early morning swim even in the depths of winter. He was also to inherit two more of his father's characteristics. John Cadbury was an active social reformer who helped rid Birmingham of the scandal of child chimney sweeps and he was also an astute salesman, being one of the first shopkeepers in the city to introduce plate glass windows to display his goods.

Like Titus Salt, George Cadbury originally wanted to be a doctor but the death of his mother when he was fourteen and his father's failing health meant that he was needed in the family firm. After attending the Friends' day school in Birmingham and serving for two years as an assistant in Joseph Rowntree senior's grocery shop in York, where Joseph junior was a fellow apprentice, he joined his father who was now concentrating on manufacturing, having transferred the shop to his nephew.

In 1847 John Cadbury's original works had been bought by the Great Western Railway and he had moved to Bridge Street near the canal. Here, with the aid of a small group of men and four ovens capable of roasting 4 tons of cocoa beans a day, he made sixteen different kinds of chocolate and eleven types of cocoa. All were made for drinking and were sold in blocks in which the ground beans were mixed with cornflour, arrowroot and other starchy substances. When sugar was added, the product was known as chocolate. Cocoa had a more bitter taste and was often sold for medicinal purposes – John Cadbury's range included both homeopathic and dietetic varieties. He also sold a small amount of 'French eating chocolate' but high prices meant that this was very much a luxury item.

Two events in 1853, shortly before George joined his father's firm, gave chocolate manufacture in general and Cadbury's in particular an important boost. In his great free trade budget W.E. Gladstone reduced the duty on imported cocoa beans to a penny a pound and so brought the price of cocoa and chocolate within the range of millions of people. At the same time John Cadbury and his brother Benjamin received a royal warrant as suppliers of cocoa to

Queen Victoria. Through the latter part of the 1850s the two brothers, with the help of George and his older brother Richard, gradually built up their manufacturing business and introduced new products like Vanilla Eating Chocolate. But progress was slow and when in 1861 John retired and transferred the management of the Bridge Street works to his two sons the firm was employing only twelve hands and making a loss.

George and Richard, both in their early twenties, committed everything that they had in an effort to keep the business going. Each had inherited £4,000 from their mother which was invested in the firm and both brothers worked long hours six days a week, turning their hand to every aspect of the work. George regularly got up at 5.15 every morning, walked home to his father's house for a frugal lunch and took a tea of bread, butter and water in the works before working on until nine in the evening. He rationed his personal spending to ten shillings a week by giving up his morning paper, tea and coffee – he was already a total abstainer from drink and tobacco. He later wrote: 'I was spending at that time for travelling, clothing, charities and everything else about £25 a year. It is just the money that I saved by living so sparely that carried us over the crisis.'

The Cadbury brothers won the respect of the workforce at Bridge Street not just because of their own sacrifices to keep the business going but also because of their concern for their employees' welfare. Despite its considerable difficulties, Cadburys was the first firm in Birmingham to introduce a half holiday on Saturday. George and Richard ran a sick club; they bought a football and a bicycle for the boy workers and when business was slack they organized games in the yard. They also introduced new products like Icelandic Moss, a mixture of cocoa and a dried lichen reputed to have health-giving properties, and Mexican chocolate, a vanilla-flavoured eating chocolate. But despite their efforts the business continued to make a loss and by 1864 the two brothers were preparing to give up and had already decided on new careers, Richard as a land surveyor and George as a tea planter in the Himalayas. In that year, however, the tide turned and the firm made a profit for the first time in four years. The recovery continued and by 1866 the workforce at Bridge Street was up to seventy. It was at this point that the Cadbury brothers took a decision which was to revolutionize the whole British chocolate industry and transform their own position in it from being one of the smallest manufacturers to the largest, using one-third of all cocoa beans imported into the country.

The cocoa produced by Cadburys, like that made by all other manufacturers in the mid-nineteenth century, was a very impure substance. It had to be heavily adulterated with starches like potato or sago flour and with treacle to counteract the strong and unpleasant taste of the cocoa butter which was found in raw beans. In 1866 George heard that a Dutch manufacturer called Van Houten had invented a machine which extracted the butter and reduced cocoa to a fine powder which could be sold unadulterated. He immediately went over to Holland and, without knowing a word of Dutch, met Van Houten and bought his machine. Later the same year Cadburys became the first British company to produce pure cocoa. It was heavily advertised on the sides of London buses and sold in tins decorated with a picture of the cocoa plant, the Royal Coat of Arms and testimonials from the medical press. Sales boomed and by 1870 the workforce at Bridge Street had increased to 200.

The success of Cadbury's Pure Cocoa Essence, as it came to be called, owed much to the Sale of Food and Drugs Act passed in 1875. This forbade manufacturers from labelling adulterated cocoa as pure cocoa and put many firms out of business. Cadburys, as the only cocoa firm in Britain which could legitimately use the word 'pure' about its products, lost no time in ramming home the message in its advertising. It concentrated particularly on stressing their health-giving properties. Early advertisements pointed out that cocoa 'is specially rich in flesh-forming and strength-sustaining principles' and 'is a gentle stimulant and sustains against hunger and bodily fatigue'. They also quoted the *Medical Times and Gazette*'s considered opinion that 'Cadbury's Cocoa Essence might be introduced into many boarding schools in lieu of the discoloured watery liquid which is served out under the misused name of tea'.

In 1874 Cadburys relinquished the tea and coffee trade to concentrate entirely on the manufacture of cocoa and chocolate. The use of the Dutch press had given a stimulus to the production of eating chocolate which was made with the extracted cocoa butter. In the late 1860s the firm started to challenge what had hitherto been a Continental monopoly by making chocolates with cream and fruit filled centres. In 1870 the first chocolate assortments were produced, packed in boxes designed by Richard with pictures of children playing, cats, flowers and other pretty and sentimental scenes. By 1876 Cadbury's range of eating chocolates included pralines, crème balls, croquettes, vanilla sticks and fruit creams.

The great increase in the numbers employed at Bridge Street did not alter the family atmosphere of the works. From the very early days George had developed the habit of breakfasting with the workers and leading them in prayers at the start of every working day. In 1866 he instituted a more formal daily service for all employees, acting partly on the suggestion of Joseph Fry who had such gatherings in his Bristol factory and pointed out that 'in addition to the religious benefit which may be looked for, there is a great advantage in bringing the workpeople once a day under review. It is often a means of observing their conduct and checking any tendency to impropriety'. The service at Cadburys, which became known as the 'Daily Reading', began with a passage of Scripture followed by a period of silence for prayer. A hymn was later added, often of the Moody and Sankey variety. George Cadbury was an enthusiast for revivalist choruses and introduced hymn singing into Friends' meetings in England. When the Daily Reading was stopped in 1870 the workers signed a petition calling for its resumption. For the next thirty years the entire Cadburys workforce gathered every morning for the service. It was usually taken by George who had walked in from his home where he had already conducted family prayers.

The daily service was not the only practice that marked Cadburys out as an unusual firm to work for. There was also a strict code of rules governing behaviour in the factory, with lapses being punished by fines which were sent to the local hospital. Spilling cocoa, chicory, flour or sugar and not gathering it up incurred a penalty of a halfpenny, as did unnecessary shouting or singing. Weighing with inaccurate scales cost each offender twopence and going into the street without good reason threepence. The most serious misdemeanour was playing with boys during work hours which carried a penalty of sixpence. The insistence on high standards both of cleanliness and personal morality seems to have paid dividends. Cadburys came to have a reputation both for its happy and well-behaved workforce and for the quality of its products and this good name extended beyond the British Isles. In 1862 the firm exhibited at the International Exhibition and shortly afterwards it opened a shop in Paris directly challenging the acknowledged kings of confectionery on their home ground.

The expansion of the firm made a move from the cramped premises at Bridge Street desirable. Like Titus Salt, George Cadbury was anxious to move his workers away from the over-crowded and polluted conditions of a city-centre factory and he also saw that transferring production to a green field site made commercial sense. In 1878 he bought $14\frac{1}{2}$ acres of meadows and woodland four miles south-west of Birmingham just off the Bristol road, with good access to both the canal and the railway network. A stream called the Bourn traversed the estate and at first George resolved to call his new factory Bournbrook. However, in deference to the popular prejudice in favour of French chocolate confectionery he changed the name to Bournville.

George moved to a nearby cottage so that he could personally supervise the construction of the new works which he had himself designed with the help of a young architect. Determined not to get into debt, he employed no contractors but hired labourers directly by the week and bought bricks by the thousand. The 320 workers who moved to Bournville in 1879 found not just a light and spacious factory complete with dining rooms and drying and changing facilities but cricket and football pitches and parkland where they could stroll and play during their lunch hour. There were also sixteen semi-detached houses provided for foremen. Later on the workers were provided with two open-air swimming pools and a full-size concert hall and lecture theatre.

Installed in their new factory, Cadburys rapidly consolidated

126

their position as the leading British chocolate manufacturer and challenged the traditional pre-eminence of the French in the confectionery industry. In 1880 Frederic Kinchelman, a master confectioner from the Continent, was engaged at Bournville to develop such lines as nougats and mints. In 1881 the firm got its first order from Australia, with South Africa and India becoming major customers shortly afterwards. As the fancy confectionery business grew, departments for making cardboard boxes, decorated tins and packing cases were added to the original chocolate factory, and by 1889 the workforce at Bournville had grown to 1,193.

Despite their growing wealth, George and Richard Cadbury continued to lead very frugal lives. Every Monday they bought a leg of mutton which provided their lunch for the next five days; it was cut into two with the larger piece served roast on Monday, cold on Tuesday and hashed or minced on Wednesday and the smaller piece served boiled on Thursday and cold on Friday. The two brothers also continued to show a very close interest in the welfare of their employees whom they liked to address by their Christian names. It was not uncommon to see them get down on their hands and knees and crawl under a table in one of the workrooms early on a winter morning to make sure that the water pipes were hot enough. Nor were they above helping out on the production lines – girls in the packing department recalled Richard making birds' nests for Easter eggs. They appointed a special engineer whose sole duty was to make the machinery in the factory safer and allowed every girl to bathe once a week in the firm's time. In 1902 Bournville became the first factory in Britain to have its own resident works doctor. Soon afterwards a dentist was installed as well and Cadburys made it a policy not to employ any boy or girl unless their parents gave written consent that their teeth should be properly attended to.

There was a distinctly paternalistic and moralistic aspect to the Cadbury brothers' rule over Bournville. Corridors were so arranged that girls and boys did not meet on their way to or from work and there were separate recreation areas for the two sexes on either side of the main road outside the factory. The girls' area was reached by a tunnel which gave direct access to a changing room so that no male could catch the merest glimpse of a gym slip or bare ankle. Cottages provided for female employees were protected by nightwatchmen, one of whose duties was to light fires in the afternoon so that the girls came home to a warm home in the evening. Girls who lived out in neighbouring villages were escorted home in convoys led by men carrying lanterns. George Cadbury refused to employ married women, believing that a wife's place was at home. He also believed that allowing married women to work encouraged their husbands to become loafers and idlers living on their wife's wages. Whenever a girl left Bournville to wed, he had a personal interview with her and presented her with a Bible and a carnation.

But if George and Richard expected their workers to comply with their strict moral code they also treated them with immense kindness and consideration. George often visited the girls in their homes and asked them to sing Moody and Sankey hymns and he also regularly went along to their lunchtime sewing classes and read to them. At leaving time on wet evenings Richard stood by the factory gates until he heard the Birmingham train approaching and then blew a whistle so that the girls could dash from the shelter of the factory and avoid a wait in the rain. In 1929 on the occasion of the fiftieth anniversary of the opening of the Bournville works sixty-three men and women who had worked for Cadburys between 1870 and 1899 set down their memories and impressions of the firm in a book which is still preserved in the company archives. It is filled with tributes to the kindness and humanity of the two partners, known universally as 'Governor Richard' and 'Governor George'. Miss Alice Bond, who joined the card box department in 1883, wrote of George: 'I was very much impressed by his personal interest in everything concerning the workpeople, not only for their physical but for their spiritual welfare. It was his object in life to lead all with whom he came into contact to the Lord he loved and served so well.' Of Richard she wrote: 'His beautiful face fit in perfectly with my ideal of what a Man of God should be. And in after years when his hair became white he was always associated in my mind with the patriarch Abraham.'

Bournville became known as the factory in the garden. It was surrounded on all sides by fields and woods and in borders outside their offices George and Richard grew roses which were sent weekly to the Grocery Exchange in Manchester to be distributed to their customers. But many of their workers were still living in the back-to-back slums of Birmingham. It was his determination to put into practice his conviction that 'no man ought to be compelled to live where a rose cannot grow' that led George to build the model village of Bournville and become a pioneer of the concept of the garden city. He was also concerned to prevent speculators moving into the area around his new factory and putting up jerry-built houses for the workers. In 1895 he bought 120 acres of land adjoining the factory and began planning a community which would not just be limited, in the manner of Saltaire, to his own employees. He acted, as he later wrote, with the object 'of alleviating the evils which arise from the insanitary and insufficient accommodation supplied to large numbers of the working classes, and of securing to the workers in factories some of the advantages of outdoor life, with opportunities for the natural and healthful occupation of cultivating the soil'.

The village which George Cadbury created at Bournville had many novel features. Perhaps the most important was the amount of open space. One tenth of the estate was reserved for public open space and the whole village was laid out so that a pedestrian could cross from one end to the other without once leaving parkland. The houses were built six to an acre and laid out in clusters following the natural contours of the land while the public buildings, shops and schools were grouped around a large common. Cadbury laid down that no house should be allowed to cover more than a quarter of the land belonging to it, thus providing every residence with a large garden which was laid out with vegetable patches, flower beds and fruit trees. The value of garden produce was estimated as the equivalent of a two-shilling saving on weekly rents for each householder and Cadbury was fond of pointing out that the Bournville villagers grew an average of £58 worth of food per acre every year where before the same land had yielded just £5 worth an acre.

Like Saltaire, Bournville had no public house and was provided with both an elementary school and a day continuation school for adults. A democratically elected council was set up to run the village's affairs. Cadbury had originally intended that the houses should be owned by their occupiers and the first 143 houses built had been sold at cost price on a 999 year lease with purchasers being given loans at $2\frac{1}{2}$ per cent interest. However, several of those who bought houses at these very advantageous terms quickly sold them at a considerable profit, and to prevent this speculation all the properties in the village were vested in a charitable trust which rented them out. The Bournville Village Trust was set up in 1901, by which time there were 370 houses on the estate. Cadbury insisted that the trust must achieve a 5 per cent profit, which was to be reinvested in the village, to prove to others that such a venture was not bound to make a loss.

As Cadbury had hoped, Bournville village became a showplace and a mecca for those interested in housing and town planning. Detailed and well-publicized research was carried out showing the benefits which living in such a spacious environment conferred on its inhabitants. The death rate in the village, at 7.7 per thousand, and the infant mortality rate, at 5.1 per cent, for example, were exactly half those prevailing in Birmingham. The example of Bournville played an important role in the creation of other garden cities like Letchworth and Welwyn in Hertfordshire. It also helped to create a much greater interest in the whole subject of town planning. Cadbury himself established a lectureship in civic design and town planning at Birmingham University and had a hand in the first Town Planning Act which was passed in Britain in 1909. He had come to appreciate earlier than most the problems of inner-city living and he spelled out a compelling and practical alternative:

Through my experience among the back streets of Birmingham I have been brought to the conclusion that it is impossible to raise a nation, morally, physically and spiritually in such surroundings, and that the only effective way is to bring men out of the cities into the country and to give to every man his garden where he can come into touch with nature and thus know more of nature's God. I believe the time will come when the race will be so enlightened as to make it illegal to build any more cities where the houses are closely packed together.

George Cadbury's concern about the plight of inner-city dwellers was born out of his lifelong involvement in the adult education movement. In 1859 at the age of twenty he became a teacher at a class for working men which met every Sunday morning in Severn Street, a particularly run-down area of Birmingham. He continued to teach there for the next fifty-two years, getting up every Sunday at 5.30 and riding either on a horse or a bicycle the five miles from his home to the school which started at seven. He usually spent all morning at the school, where he taught Scripture and basic literacy, before riding back to the Bournville works for a simple lunch of biscuits and raisins and then going on to a Friends' Meeting in the firm's dining room. On weekday evenings, after a day in the office which might not end until 9 p.m., he often visited the young men from his class in their homes. Altogether he taught more than 7,000 men many of whom, fired by his example, went on themselves to become teachers. He was delighted to find on a visit to a Church of England Sunday School in one of the poorest parts of Birmingham that twelve of the fourteen teachers had been members of his class.

His experience in the Severn Street School persuaded George Cadbury that moral exhortation alone was not sufficient to improve the circumstances of the working man. 'It is not enough to talk to him about ideals', he wrote. 'How can he cultivate ideals when his home is a slum and his only possible place of recreation the public house? Some people would leave the people in their degrading surroundings while they discussed their moral and spiritual theories about raising them. To win them to better ideals you must give them better conditions of life. The material and the spiritual react on each other.' Putting these principles into practice, he acquired a public house which had caused the police more trouble than any other in Birmingham and turned it into a working men's club. He also gave strong support to the adult education movement. Employees at Bournville wishing to better themselves were allowed to leave work an hour early twice a week to attend night school. In 1894 he established Selly Oak Institute a mile or so from the Bournville works as an educational centre for working men.

George Cadbury's commitment to adult education led him to found five colleges at Selly Oak where men and women could study and put into practice the Christian social gospel to which he was so attached. The first was Woodbroke, established in 1902 in the house where he himself had lived from 1880 to 1894 as 'a place where spiritual and intellectual stimulus, combined with experience in Christian social work, can be obtained'. Woodbroke was to be an interdenominational settlement and reflected George's strong belief in Christian unity and the coming together of all men and women of faith to live out the beliefs which they held in common. He also hoped that it would act as a centre for the regeneration of Quakerism which he felt was in danger of losing its initial idealism and vigour and becoming flabby. The other colleges that Cadbury set up were Westhill, for Sunday School teachers, Kingsmead and Carey Hill for training missionaries, and Fircroft, established in 1909 as a residential college for working men and administered by a committee drawn from the Workers' Educational Association, the Co-operative movement and the trade unions. The five institutions were brought together in a federation known as the Selly Oak Colleges and still thrive today.

George Cadbury's generosity also extended to children. While living at Woodbroke he had a large tent in the garden where he gave tea parties for children from inner Birmingham. When in 1894 he moved to the manor house at Northfield, slightly further out along the Bristol road, he erected a building known as 'The Barn' which held 700 and was used for daily tea parties for city children. George himself attended these parties whenever he could. Altogether about 25,000 children were entertained there every year and enjoyed games of cricket and swims which were undertaken in batches of fifty boys or girls at a time – as at Bournville mixed bathing was not permitted. George built a house called 'The Beeches' in Bournville village as a summer holiday centre for children from poor families. They were weighed on arrival and departure and found to have put on an average of two-and-three-quarter pounds during their fortnight's stay, thanks partly, no doubt, to the bags of sweets which George liberally distributed whenever he visited the home. He also built a home for crippled children nearby at Woodlands which he visited every Sunday evening armed with a further plentiful supply of chocolates.

During the winter months The Beeches was used as a convalescent and rest home for Salvation Army officers. George Cadbury had enormous respect for the work of the Salvation Army as he had for all those who combined Christian missionary activity and practical social work. He joined William Lever in financing an experiment by the London Missionary Society to develop the industries of New Guinea in the interests of the natives and prevent their exploitation by outside commercial interests. In this as in all his philanthropic ventures he was strongly supported by his second wife, Elizabeth, whom he had married in 1888 following the death of his first wife, Mary.

George Cadbury's practical Christianity led naturally to involvement in politics. He was a keen Liberal and exerted much influence as president of the North Worcestershire Liberal Council. With his strong interest in social reform, Cadbury belonged to the radical wing of the party and he strongly supported the almost socialistic programme of municipal improvement carried out in Birmingham in the mid-1870s by Joseph Chamberlain. In 1878 he was himself elected to Birmingham Town Council against a Conservative candidate backed by the brewers who supplied free beer to voters. But he retired after a year and resisted attempts by W. E. Gladstone in 1892 and Lord Rosebery three years later to persuade him to stand for Parliament. He believed that his calling was to religious and social service rather than active politics. He strongly supported the Liberal programme of free trade and land reform in the 1906 election and was an enthusiastic supporter of old age pensions and the programme of higher death duties and greater taxation of the rich contained in Lloyd George's famous People's Budget. But when his friend the Liberal prime minister Henry Campbell-Bannerman offered him a privy councillorship in 1907 he turned it down, saying 'I fully feel the honour offered, but do not think it would be in the interests of the poor suffering people whose cause you and I are pleading for me to accept it'.

George Cadbury once commented: 'I have no interest in the Liberal Party except in so far as it promotes the interest of the millions of my fellow countrymen who are on or below the poverty line.' While he never gave up his allegiance to the Liberals, he found himself throughout the 1900s and 1910s becoming increasingly in sympathy with the Labour cause. He believed strongly in the need for more working-class representatives in Parliament and gave financial support to many Labour MPs. He hoped that the infant Labour Party would join the radical wing of the Liberals in a progressive alliance which would redistribute wealth in Britain and substantially help the poorer elements in society by establishing a welfare state.

Like all Quakers, he felt particularly strongly about the issue of war and peace. His dislike of militarism and jingoism came to a head during the Boer War of 1899 to 1902. He refused to tender for supplying the British troops with chocolate and cocoa, and when Queen Victoria commanded him to supply tins of chocolate with her portrait on the lid as her Christmas present to the troops in South Africa he obeyed only on condition that the firm did not make any profit out of the royal order. He paid for the printing and distribution of a million leaflets produced by the National Arbitration League and calling for an end to the war and was horrified at the new-found imperialism of many in the Liberal Party and much of the Liberal press. When the *Daily News*, the great Liberal paper which had been owned by Samuel Morley, switched to a pro-war line, Cadbury arranged for a special train to bring copies of the *Morning Leader*, the only remaining anti-war daily, to the Midlands cities. Later, in response to a plea from Lloyd George, he bought the *Daily News* so that it could become once again the organ of Liberal radicalism and pacifism.

Cadbury bought the *Daily News* on two conditions – that it would carry no betting advertisements or racing news and no advertisements for liquor. He was himself a strict teetotaller and fervent supporter of the temperance cause and in common with all Nonconformists he strongly disapproved of gambling. In 1910, nine years after his purchase of the *Daily News*, in a joint venture with Joseph Rowntree he bought two more papers, the *Morning Leader* and the *Star*, which were in financial difficulties and in danger of being taken over by someone who would end their traditionally radical stance. To the outrage of several Nonconformists the two Quakers did not insist that the *Star* should give up the racing news which had long been one of its most popular features. Cadbury defended their decision on the grounds that 'It seemed evident that the *Star* with betting and pleading for social reform and peace was far better than the *Star* (still with betting news) opposing social reform and stirring up strife with neighbouring nations'.

In 1911 Cadbury merged the *Daily News* and the *Morning Leader* and formed a charitable trust to run the new combined paper, which kept the title the *Daily News*, with his son Edward as its first chairman. 'I desire', he wrote, 'that it may be of service in bringing the ethical teaching of Jesus Christ to bear upon National questions and in promoting National Righteousness; for example that arbitration should take the place of war, and that the spirit of the Sermon on the Mount – especially of the Beatitudes – should take the place of Imperialism and of the military spirit.' True to this principle, Cadbury had already put the *Daily News* in the forefront of a number of social and political campaigns. When depression hit the London docks in 1905 the paper had launched an appeal which raised £18,000 in money and goods for the relief of those worst affected and had organized work schemes for the unemployed. The following year the paper sponsored an exhibition which drew attention to the evils of sweated industries and led directly to the first statutory minimum wage legislation in Britain. The *Daily News* also campaigned vigorously for better old age pensions, state ownership of coal mines and more public works to reduce unemployment. The paper lost Cadbury between £20,000 and £30,000 a year but, as he told his sons, he had not become a newspaper proprietor to make money but rather as an extension of his general philanthropy:

I had a profound conviction that money spent on charities was of infinitely less value than money spent in trying to arouse my fellow countrymen to the necessity for measures to ameliorate the condition of the poor, forsaken and downtrodden masses which can be done most effectively by a great newspaper.

Although philanthropy and public campaigns took up an increasing amount of his time, George Cadbury continued to go to his office at Bournville virtually every day, walking in from his home to take the morning reading at the works. In 1900 the service was made thrice weekly with a third of the 3,000-strong workforce attending each time (the most that the largest hall at Bournville could accommodate). But in 1911 the morning readings were made more frequent again in response to employees' pleas. George frequently gave a short address to the assembled workforce after leading them in a rousing hymn or chorus. Spiritually and physically his vigour showed no sign of diminishing. He took up tennis when he was nearly fifty and golf when he was seventy.

Sadly, Richard Cadbury was not as robust as his younger brother and while visiting the Holy Land in 1899 he succumbed to a fatal attack of diphtheria. Following his death the firm which the two brothers had run for 38 years became a private limited company with George as chairman, and two of his eleven children, Edward and George, as directors together with Richard's two sons, Barrow and William. Business continued to boom: by 1900 the Bournville works were three times the size of the original factory put up in 1879, and the firm was consuming 16,880 tons of raw cocoa and selling over £1 million's worth of chocolate a year. In 1897 Cadburys, which had hitherto produced only dark eating chocolate of the kind made on the Continent, manufactured a milk chocolate for the first time. Produced with powdered milk, it was not a great success. But in 1905 the firm put on sale a light milk chocolate made with fresh milk. Cadbury's Dairy Milk has continued to be one of the most popular chocolate bars in Britain ever since. The following year a slightly spiced dark chocolate called 'Bournville' was put on the market.

The spectacular success of these two new brands led Cadburys

136

to extend their operations and gain more control over the supply of their raw materials. In 1908 the firm started buying agencies in West Africa and two years later the first shipment of cocoa beans arrived from Ghana which was destined to become the major supplier of their most important raw material. Three years later, in order to prevent milk going sour before it reached the factory, the firm bought a milk-condensing plant at Knighton on the Shropshire–Staffordshire border. Similar plants were later opened in Gloucestershire, Herefordshire and Denbighshire from which condensed milk was taken by canal or rail to Bournville. In 1912 Cadburys became a public company. Some 200,000 £1 preference shares were offered to the public, with priority being given to customers and employees, and all the ordinary shares were kept in the hands of the family. Two years later the firm introduced its Plain Tray and Milk Tray boxed assortments, so called because the chocolates were arranged on cardboard trays.

By 1919 Cadbury's turnover was more than £8.1 million and Bournville was the largest chocolate factory in the world. It was also one of the most democratically managed, with a system of elected works councils on which the 7,500 employees and the management were given equal representation. The year 1919 also saw the takeover by Cadburys of Frys, the oldest chocolate manufacturers in Britain, which had effectively been run from 1855 to 1913 by George Cadbury's near-contemporary and close friend, Joseph Storrs Fry. George himself, though now eighty, continued to take an active interest in the company's affairs and attended no less than eighty-one of the ninety-two board and management committee meetings held in 1920. Part of the secret of his longevity and activity in old age was undoubtedly the simple lifestyle which he continued to practise. His homes were comfortable rather than grand. To the last he refused to spend more than a minimum on their decoration. When a visitor commented on the poor quality of the pictures, he replied, 'Why should I hang fortunes on my walls while there is so much misery in the world?'

George Cadbury died peacefully on 24 October 1922 just as the five o'clock bell sounded the end of the day shift at Bournville. The following day a two-minute silence was observed throughout the factory at 11 a.m. by the day workers and at 9.30 p.m. by the night shift. More than 16,000 people attended a memorial service on the village green during which George's favourite hymn tunes were played on the 48-bell carillon which he had erected beside the elementary school.

George Cadbury's whole life was a shining example of Christian idealism and prophetic vision translated into practical action. Asked once what his favourite quotation was, he replied 'Whatsoever thy hand findeth to do, do it with all thy might'. He himself fully lived up to that injunction. His dream of a garden city where men and women 'could breathe pure air and be elevated by the influence of trees and flowers' has been turned into a reality at Bournville which is now a thriving community of more than 7,000 homes and continues to inspire architects and town planners. Many of the economic and social reforms for which he campaigned so tirelessly have now been implemented. But perhaps it is the example he set throughout his business career as a kind employer and a scrupulously honest trader that is most relevant today. George Cadbury had no time for those men who spend the morning and noon of their lives making money and the evening giving it away, nor for those who keep their business and philanthropic activities in separate and well-insulated compartments. He believed that it was just as important that money should be made rightly as that it should be spent rightly and that the highest ideals of Christian charity and service should guide and inform every transaction on this earth. He himself lived out those ideals to the full and in a spirit of genuine and utter humility. When he was offered an honorary degree at Birmingham University in recognition of his outstanding contribution to the life of the city he turned it down saying 'I have only done what is the duty of every employer and Christian citizen'.

Since its merger with Schweppes in 1969 Cadburys has become one of the giants of the British food industry. It has remained a family firm – George's grandsons Dominic and Adrian are respectively the chief executive and the chairman of the board. Bournville remains the main manufacturing centre and now employs 4,700 people making such perennial favourites as

Cadbury's Dairy Milk and Fruit and Nut bars, Roses chocolates and Milk Tray assortments. Although the names would be familiar to George should he return to the factory today, the production techniques would certainly not be. Bournville has some of the most automated confectionery production lines in the world, each of which can manufacture and wrap 1,500 chocolate bars a minute supervised by just a handful of people. They are in operation twenty-four hours a day and turn out a total of 1,500 tons of chocolate a week, rather more than ten times the total annual production of chocolate in Britain as a whole in the year that George Cadbury was born.

8
JOSEPH ROWNTREE
(1836–1925)

Joseph Rowntree resembled his fellow Quaker and confectioner George Cadbury in many ways, not least in his combination of brilliant commercial acumen and great generosity of spirit. He too transformed a small family firm into a giant enterprise. When he joined his brother's cocoa, chocolate and chicory works in 1869 it had just twelve employees. By the time of his retirement fifty-four years later, the firm's workforce numbered more than seven thousand. Rowntree followed Cadbury in manufacturing pure chocolate, relocating his factory to an out-of-town site and establishing a model village. But in his views on industrial democracy and on philanthropy he was, if anything, perhaps a little in advance of his great friend and rival. Indeed, several of his ideas on industrial and social organization have yet to be tried or implemented and it is appropriate that a good many radical pressure groups and social experiments today are funded by the three trusts which he established.

Joseph Rowntree came from a family of Quaker grocers. His grandfather had a shop in Scarborough and his father ran a business in the centre of York. It was in a room above his father's shop that Joseph was born in 1836. He must have been conscious of the bustle below from an early age. The shop was open six days a week from six in the morning until half past eight at night. There was also a good deal of activity in the cramped quarters where Joseph and his two brothers and two sisters grew up. Two young apprentices lived with the family above the shop. On days when quarterly Meetings of the Society of Friends were held in York, up to eight visitors would stay with the Rowntrees and Joseph and his brothers would vacate their beds and sleep on the floor. When he was nine the family moved to a more spacious house just outside the city wall, but the stream of visitors and the atmosphere of high-minded discussion continued.

Joseph went to the Friends' school at Bootham in York and at sixteen he joined the apprentices in his father's shop where he learned the skills of blending tea and coffee, weighing out sugar and flour from sacks and cutting cheese and butter from the long blocks in which they arrived from farms. George Cadbury was also an apprentice in the shop and it was at this time that the close friendship between the two men was forged. In 1857 Joseph was sent to London to work in a large wholesale grocers in Fenchurch Street where he learned the art of tasting tea and coffee brought in by brokers. In the evenings he went to the House of Commons and sat in the gallery listening to the debates. He was particularly impressed by the speeches of William Ewart Gladstone and of Richard Cobden, the great apostle of free trade.

After only four months in London Joseph was summoned back to York by his father who was anxious about the effects that the bright city lights might be having on him. He continued his apprenticeship in the shop, and on the sudden death of his father later that year he took over its management with his elder brother, John. Five years later Joseph married Julia Seebohm, the daughter of a German Quaker who had settled in Bradford. Sadly, she died when they had been married for only thirteen months and shortly after giving birth to a daughter. Joseph responded to the loss of his wife by devoting more and more time to the shop, working on accounts long into the night, and by throwing himself into good works and embarking on a detailed study of poverty in York. He also took an increasingly active role in Quaker affairs, taking over his father's position on the committee which ran the Friends' schools in York and attending the yearly Meetings in London. In 1867 he married Emma Antoinette Seebohm, a cousin of his first wife, who was to bear him six children.

In 1869, at the age of thirty-three, Joseph left the shop where he had worked since leaving school and which had been his home as a young child and joined his younger brother, Henry Isaac, who had taken over a cocoa, chocolate and chicory factory in an area of York beside the River Ouse and known as Tanner's Moat. The business was experiencing some difficulties and Joseph was brought in to supervise and improve the accounts while Henry Isaac oversaw the manufacture of the firm's two main products, Superior Rock Cocoa, a blend of sugar and cocoa which was compressed into a cake and sold for ninepence a pound wholesale, and Homeopathic Cocoa which was made with added arrowroot. The factory, which produced just 12 hundredweight of cocoa a week, was very like John Cadbury's Bridge Street works in Birmingham. The premises were cramped and the technology rudimentary. Orders were delivered by a donkey which was kept in stables at the back. The firm's twelve employees took their turn at grinding and roasting cocoa beans, mixing the resulting powder with sugar to form chocolate and helping with the paperwork. There was little distinction between manual and clerical staff. Applicants for jobs in the office were asked if they could carry a 10-stone bag of flour and often found themselves hauling sacks of sugar and cocoa around the works.

As at Cadburys, a family atmosphere pervaded the Tanner's Moat works. The system of payment was delightfully trusting. Each employee kept a note of his own hours of work and at the end of the week the general foreman went round with a hat full of coins and asked everyone in turn: 'How much time has thee got?' The small office in which Joseph worked had a trap door in the floor which he opened if he wished to talk to anyone in the counting-house below and through which he dropped letters for posting. Both brothers took a strong interest in their employees' welfare. They took round pork pies and cups of cocoa to those working late in the evenings and were always ready to listen to anyone with a problem or worry. Hours and wages were much the same as in other local factories, 6 a.m. to 6 p.m. on Mondays to Fridays and 6 a.m. to 2 p.m. on Saturdays, with girls of fourteen starting at three shillings a week and the best-paid men getting eighteen shillings, but word soon got round York that Rowntrees was a good place to work.

Although Henry Isaac introduced new lines like Icelandic Moss and Farinaceous cocoa and chocolate drops and creams, the business continued to make a small trading loss. Part of the reason was the brothers' insistence on applying strict Quaker principles in commercial matters. Joseph refused to engage in any advertising and he was firmly opposed to making any claims about the firm's products which were not absolutely accurate. When a local grocer put a somewhat extravagant label on his packets of Rowntree's Homeopathic Cocoa he reacted angrily: 'It is not a pure ground cocoa. It is not produced from the finest Trinidad Nuts. It is not the "best for family use". In fact the whole thing is a sham, not very creditable to anyone concerned with it.' In the long run Joseph Rowntree's insistence on honesty and high standards was to pay dividends but in the short run it was something of a liability. By the mid-1870s the firm was making an annual trading loss of £500 and the two brothers were wondering how they could keep it going.

The saviour of the company was a Frenchman called Claude Gaget who called in at the Tanner's Moat works in 1879 with samples of gums and pastilles which he had made. The French had an effective monopoly of the manufacture of these types of confectionery and no British firm had attempted to break it. The Rowntree brothers decided to try their hand and bought Gaget's recipe and a large boiling pot in which to make the fruit gums. In 1881 they produced their first batch of 'Crystallised Gum Pastilles' which retailed for a penny an ounce. The pastilles were a considerable success and more workers were taken on to produce them. However, the firm was still making a loss in the early 1880s and suffered a severe blow in 1883 when Henry Isaac died suddenly of peritonitis at the age of forty-five. Joseph was now left on his own to run the ailing business.

The continuing success of the fruit gums and pastilles gradually brought about a permanent improvement in the fortunes of the firm. By 1885 4 tons of these sweets were being manufactured every week and the workforce had increased to 200. Two years later a horse-drawn lorry was taking the firm's daily output to the railway station, a far cry from the donkey of earlier days. The Tanner's Moat works was still very ramshackle and unsuited to large-scale factory production. There was no lift in the main six-storey building and heavy sacks had to be humped up and down stairs. Joseph bought up adjoining cottages and stables and extended the original premises. Possibly under the influence of his son, John Wilhelm, who began work in the factory in 1885 at the age of seventeen, he also dropped his earlier opposition to advertising and in 1886 discreet notices commending Rowntree's confectionery appeared in the popular magazines *Tit-Bits* and *Answers*. Between 1883 and 1886 the firm's annual sales doubled to £110,000.

Lack of capital delayed Rowntree's introduction of the Dutch cocoa press which had transformed Cadbury's business in the late 1860s. Joseph went to Holland in 1877 to look at Van Houten's machine and he went on holiday in Switzerland that year with George Cadbury where the new process was almost certainly discussed. But it was not until 1887 that the cocoa press was introduced at Tanner's Moat. In that year Rowntree took on a Dutchman, Cornelius Hollander, who was installed in rooms at the top of an old flour mill. An iron door and padlock were fitted to safeguard the secrecy of his experiments. Soon he had produced an absolutely pure cocoa powder which was put on the market under the brand name 'elect'. It was heavily promoted and advertised. In 1892 Rowntrees took full-page advertisements in the daily papers which included coupons that could be exchanged in shops for a sample of the cocoa and an unused penny stamp. They were headed 'A cup of cocoa and your morning paper for nothing'. The new 'elect' cocoa proved an even more successful innovation than the fruit gums and pastilles and by 1894 the firm was in a highly profitable state and employing nearly 900 people.

Joseph Rowntree was worried that this great expansion would destroy the family atmosphere of the firm and make it difficult for him to help employees on an individual basis. He had already experienced two setbacks in his efforts to promote the welfare of the workforce which showed the difference in attitude between those engaged in a small family concern and employees in a large business. In 1885 he set up a Cocoa Works Debating Society. A similar venture which he had established among the apprentices in his father's shop had been very successful, but in the more

144

impersonal atmosphere of the factory the idea of debates and discussion among the workers had little appeal and the society was a failure. In the same year he organized an outing to the Yorkshire coast for the entire workforce. The plan was that those who wished would leave the specially chartered train at Goathland and tramp across the North York moors to Whitby where they would join the rest of the party. Unfortunately the weather was bad and the walkers were soaked when they got to the seaside town. They found the pubs warm and welcoming and some got so drunk that they had to be escorted by the police back on to the train in the evening. Joseph, who was himself an ardent teetotaller, was very shaken by this behaviour and there were no more works outings for some time, although he continued to organize concerts and to invite office staff for social evenings at his home.

Like Jeremiah Colman and George Cadbury, Joseph Rowntree took a fatherly attitude towards the many girls who worked in his factory. In 1891 he appointed a welfare officer to attend to their health and their behaviour. She laid down that girls must come to work in black dresses. Blouses and skirts were forbidden after one young girl appeared in a blouse the collar of which failed to cover her throat. She was reprimanded with the comment 'This might draw a man's attention to you'. As well as keeping a strict eye on their attire, the welfare officer also ran a lending library and organized social events for the girls, visited them at home when they were ill and acted as a confidante and adviser.

By now Joseph had come to feel that the greatest service he could do his workforce was to move his factory out of the centre of York. Like Salt and Cadbury he was motivated by both humanitarian and commercial considerations in deciding to relocate his works. The premises at Tanner's Moat were hopelessly crowded and lacked amenities like a canteen or rest room. They were also totally unsuitable for efficient manufacturing and distribution. In 1890 Rowntree bought 29 acres of land on the Haxby Road to the north-east of the city and set about building a new factory which would be light, airy and spacious. The move from Tanner's Moat to the new premises began five years later and was not completed until 1910.

As with Cadburys at Bournville, the move to Haxby Road enabled Rowntrees greatly to expand their business. In 1897 the firm
became a limited liability company with Joseph as chairman and
his two eldest sons, John Wilhelm and Seebohm, as directors along
with Henry Isaac's son, Francis, John's son, Arnold, and J.B.
Morrell, a fellow Quaker. By now the number of employees had
reached 1,000. It climbed to 2,000 in 1902 and to 4,000 in 1906, by
which time the weekly production of 'elect' cocoa was more than 26
tons. Advertising, which came under the control of Arnold, was
increased and the firm went in for some bold publicity stunts like
fitting a giant replica cocoa tin to one of the earliest motor vehicles
in Yorkshire, and displaying a barge covered with advertisements
and drawn by a mechanically propelled swan at the Oxford and
Cambridge boat race.

Joseph deplored such vulgarity but accepted the need for it in
the increasingly competitive climate of the early twentieth
century. Although now in his mid-sixties he continued to run the
firm although he delegated much of the day-to-day decision making
to his fellow directors and to the departmental managers, most of
whom he had promoted from the shop floor. Increasingly his own
interest lay with the welfare and morale of the workforce. He was
more and more concerned about the growing polarization between
capital and labour and the alienation of employees in large industrial organizations like his own. In 1902 in an effort to bridge the
gap he set up the *Cocoa Works Magazine*, one of the first house
journals in Britain. At the same time he instituted prizes for
suggestions to improve methods of production and packaging of
goods and conditions of work in the factory. He hoped that these
would help to hold employees' interest in their work. In the first
issue of the new journal he wrote:

The increasing number of those who are associated with the
Cocoa Works makes it impossible to keep up a personal
acquaintance with the staff as fully as was the case in the earlier
years of the business. This change, I know, is inevitable. But if
the business is to accomplish all that the Directors desire in
combining social progress with commercial success, the entire

146

body of workers must be animated by a common aim, and this will surely be furthered by a periodical devoted to matters of common interest.

Numerous welfare schemes were introduced in the new factory and Joseph was the driving force behind most of them. In 1904 he laid on free medical and dental facilities. By now there were seven full-time welfare workers. In 1905 a domestic school was started in the works to teach the girls the principles of managing a home. Those under seventeen were obliged to attend and their time was paid for by the firm. Two years later classes were laid on for the boys in physical training, maths and English with similar conditions applying. These day continuation classes continued until the 1960s. In 1906 Joseph started one of the first occupational pension schemes in Britain. He himself put £10,000 into the pension fund and the firm put in a further £9,000. Employees' contributions varied from 2 to 5 per cent of wages and the company put in thirty shillings for every £1 paid in by men and up to £3 for every £1 paid in by women.

Joseph Rowntree's most ambitious welfare project was the creation of the model village of New Earswick on 123 acres of land which he bought in 1901 adjoining the Haxby Road factory. Like George Cadbury, he was determined to create a mixed community of manual and white-collar workers which was not restricted just to those who worked in his factory. He engaged as architect Raymond Unwin, one of the pioneers of town planning and the garden city concept, and told him to provide dwellings 'artistic in appearance, sanitary, well-built, and yet within the means of men earning about 25 shillings a week'. There were to be no more than twelve houses to an acre, each must have a garden with two fruit trees and all living rooms must face the sun. The village was governed by an elected village council which met in the Folk Hall opened by Joseph in 1907. The hall also provided facilities for debating, music, adult education and accommodation for the services of different religious denominations, a deliberate ecumenical gesture to counter the sectarianism of having different buildings for worship put up by individual Churches.

147

Among the stipulations which Rowntree made in the deed which established the New Earswick Village Trust in 1904 was that none of the buildings in the village should be used for the manufacture, distribution or sale of intoxicating liquor. The evils of drink had come to assume an increasing importance in his thinking. In 1897 he had collaborated with Arthur Sherwell, later a Liberal MP, on a book entitled *The Temperance Problem and Social Reform*. It pointed out that working men spent an average of one-sixth of their income on drink and argued that without greater temperance social problems such as poverty would not be solved. Rowntree believed that the root of the problem lay in the fact that the drink trade was governed by the profit motive. He believed that Britain should either effectively nationalize the retail liquor trade by handing it over to local authorities or introduce the company system operating in Norway and parts of Sweden where bars were run by managers on fixed salaries.

Joseph Rowntree was keen to see people's palaces established as alternatives to public houses along the lines of Samuel Morley's efforts at the Old Vic Theatre. He suggested that there should be one in each town, financed through the profits of the drink trade and combining the functions of art gallery, concert hall and temperance café. He hoped that they would become places where young men and women would do their courting. At the same time he advocated making pubs less attractive by allowing no female bartenders to be employed. He also called for much higher taxation on drink.

Rowntree's position on drink may seem severe but it derived from personal experience of the evils that alcohol could do and from his deep compassion for the plight of the poor and neglected in society. He himself knew a town clerk of York who was so addicted to drink that he frequently attended committees in a state of complete intoxication and a city surveyor who was generally in a stupor under the table at the end of the Lord Mayor's banquets. In a moving memorandum written in 1914 he begged his children to abstain from excessive drinking and admitted how easily he himself could have succumbed to it. He pointed out that there was hardly a family in Britain which did not have a relative who had been ruined by drink. Rowntree took up the temperance cause so strongly not out of a puritanical wish to stop people enjoying themselves – although he himself was a complete teetotaller he never advocated a total prohibition of alcohol – but because he saw excessive drinking as the greatest obstacle standing in the way of social progress.

He realized all too well that what made public houses so attractive to many working men was the squalor of their homes and the monotony of their work. Those evils had to be tackled just as much as the evil of drink. His concern with poverty and its amelioration dated back to a visit to Ireland which he had made in his teens with his father in the midst of the terrible potato famine when he had seen men and women lying dead by the roadside. To escape despair and self-pity after his first wife's death he had busied himself in collecting statistics about the extent of poverty, illiteracy and crime in York. Many of the figures which he collected were used by his son Seebohm in his seminal study, *Poverty – A Study in Town Life*, published in 1901, which showed that over 27 per cent of the total population of York, and 43 per cent of those in the wage-earning class, lived at or below the poverty line.

For Rowntree collecting statistics and writing about poverty was not enough. He was also determined to work towards its eradication. He was active in politics, being founder and chairman of the York Liberal Association and a fervent supporter of the radical Liberalism which laid the foundations of the British Welfare State. He wrote a powerful pamphlet calling for the abolition of the House of Lords when it was holding up Liberal legislation on old age pensions and national insurance and was sympathetic to the emerging Labour Party and a close friend of its leader, Ramsay MacDonald. He was also a philanthropist on a large scale and gave away thousands of pounds. Initially he practised a fairly conventional form of charity, bestowing his bounty on deserving causes and individuals in need. But he came to feel that what he called 'the charity of endowment, the charity of emotion, the charity that takes the place of justice' was condescending and often did more harm than good. Like Andrew Carnegie he developed his own philosophy of giving which rested almost as

149

much on a conviction of the evil of holding on to wealth as on the beneficial effects to be produced by its distribution. Rowntree believed that he held his own wealth on trust and he also felt that it was desirable that rich individuals should spend all their money during their own lifetimes. However, he found himself with a large accumulation of wealth late on in life and the practical question arose as to how this could best be applied to secure the kind of results which he wished to see.

Rowntree found the answer in the creation of three trusts which he established in 1904 and to which he committed half his wealth. Each had a distinct purpose. The Joseph Rowntree Village Trust was to run New Earswick and promote experiments and reforms in the areas of housing and living conditions, the Joseph Rowntree Charitable Trust was to fund social research, adult education and Quaker projects, and the Joseph Rowntree Social Service Trust was to support social and political work which could not be funded by a charitable body. In a memorandum addressed to his children Joseph explained the thinking that underlay his choice of tasks for the three trusts:

> I feel that much current philanthropic effort is directed to remedying the more superficial manifestations of social evils or distress, while little thought or effort is directed to search out the underlying causes of such evils or distress. Obvious distress or evil generally evokes so much feeling that the necessary agencies for alleviating it are pretty adequately supported. It is much easier to obtain funds for the famine-stricken people in India than to originate and carry through a searching enquiry into the causes of these recurring famines. The soup kitchen in York never has difficulty in obtaining adequate financial support, but an enquiry into the extent and causes of poverty would enlist very little support.

Rowntree singled out certain specific areas which he hoped that his trusts would fund. They included research on temperance, land reform and world peace, helping political organizations and pressure groups facing financial difficulty and maintaining the purity of elections in York, if necessary by bringing prosecutions against offenders. His commitment to this last aim resulted from direct personal experience. As a young man he had been horrified to see a tradesman sitting in his shop doorway after a municipal election with a bowl of half-crowns beside him and paying out coins to those who had voted for him. He had also once been approached by a beggar who told him that the £3 he had been given for his vote had been stolen.

Through his trusts Rowntree hoped to get at the root of contemporary social problems by identifying and tackling their underlying causes rather than simply alleviating their symptoms. He was particularly concerned about the hold that 'selfish and unscrupulous wealth' had over public opinion through the press and expressed the hope that his trusts would buy and control newspapers, 'conducting them not with a primary view to profit but with the object of influencing public thought in the right channels'. In 1904, on his suggestion, the Social Service Trust took over ownership of the *Northern Echo*, the long-established Darlington-based Liberal daily paper which circulated throughout north-east England. This was the beginning of an interest in provincial newspapers which was eventually to take in sixteen titles and to lead to the formation of the Westminster Press group. In 1907 the trust helped to launch the *Nation*, a journal founded by a group of young Liberals which was later merged with the *New Statesman*, and three years later in a joint venture with George Cadbury it acquired the *Morning Leader* and the *Star*.

In 1907 Rowntree wrote another memorandum for his children outlining his attitude to wealth. It gives a fascinating insight into his character. 'The observation of a life-time', he wrote,

> has led to the belief that any considerable amount of wealth more often proves a curse than a blessing. .... I know how easy it is to acquire expensive habits which, so far from increasing the real richness and fulness of life, add to its burden. One of the mischievous ways in which these expensive habits tell is by increasing the barrier between wealthy people and their fellows. It lessens that realizing sense of human brotherhood, which it is of such paramount moment to maintain.

He enjoined his children to cultivate a simple lifestyle and abstain from luxuries.

His own life was a model in this respect. He lived modestly in York throughout his adult life, first in his parents' house in Bootham and then at Clifton Lodge on the outskirts of the city. His one indulgence was an annual holiday in Switzerland in which he pursued his great love of walking and climbing. He kept himself fit through regular exercise and was still happily climbing 1,000 ft mountains at the age of seventy-eight. Regularity was, indeed, the keynote of Rowntree's life. He kept to a strict routine from which he never deviated. Every Saturday, for example, he took the ten o'clock train from York to Scarborough where he had a cup of coffee in his cousin's café and bought some apples and ginger biscuits before setting off for a walk along the cliffs. At four o'clock he returned to the café for tea before taking the train home. For company on these walks, which he began in early middle age and continued until just before his death, he took with him a member of his adult class, an employee with a particular problem or worry or one of his managers with whom he wished to discuss some business matter.

Despite his misgivings about the possession of wealth Rowntree did accept that it added to a person's potential usefulness to society. He suggested that after passing through the useful discipline of mastering the details of a business or profession his children should enter upon some public work or personal effort on behalf of others. Once again, he had shown the way in his own life. He had, indeed, devoted himself to the welfare of others long before he had properly established his business and become a wealthy man himself. At the age of twenty-one he began taking a regular Sunday morning literacy and Scripture class in an adult school, a practice which he continued for the next forty years.

At the end of his 1907 memorandum Rowntree expressed a more general concern about wealth. He wrote: 'the enormous increase of wealth which has come to the country since the introduction of machinery has not been at all evenly distributed over the population and the share of the great body of workers has been inadequate'. He argued that the share of profits in industrial enterprises which went to labour should be increased and that going to capital diminished. The twin themes of fairer distribution of wealth and industrial democracy came to dominate both Rowntree's thinking and his actions in the last two decades of his life. His firm was one of the first in Britain to establish minimum wage rates and provide pensions for all employees. After the annual shareholders' meeting he held another meeting for all employees at which a much fuller survey of the year's work was given and questions were invited. He saw this as the first step towards creating a much closer partnership between capital and labour.

Substantial progress in the field of worker participation was made at Rowntrees in Joseph's last five years as chairman. During the First World War elected works councils were set up in each department and given considerable powers to alter conditions of work. In 1919 they voted for complete closure of the factory on Saturday with longer hours being worked from Monday to Friday in lieu. In the same year every worker was given a week's paid holiday every year. In 1921 an appeal committee was formed with two members elected by the workforce, two chosen by the directors and a chairman appointed by the committee. Any employee who felt aggrieved by a disciplinary decision could appeal to the committee which had the power to reduce or increase the penalty imposed by management. In 1923 every workman was given a say in the appointment of the foreman of his department. In the same year Joseph finally won a long battle with his fellow directors and a profit-sharing scheme was introduced.

In 1923 Joseph, who was now eighty-seven, retired from the chairmanship of Rowntrees and handed over to his son, Seebohm. The struggling firm which he had joined fifty-four years earlier now had annual profits of over £100,000, a turnover of £3.2 million and a workforce of 7,000. Even more important for Joseph, it was run on the principles of justice and fairness and had a level of worker participation in both decision making and profits which was far in advance of virtually every other company in the country. After his retirement, Joseph continued to go to the works most days and continued to take his weekly walk at Scarborough on Saturdays. One morning in February 1925 he was in his office at the factory writing some notes on John Bright, the Quaker politician and pacifist whose speeches had so impressed him in his youth. He complained of feeling cold and was persuaded to go home to bed. Five days later he died.

Joseph's sons continued to run the business in much the same spirit as their father. The last member of the family to serve on the board was Seebohm's son, Peter, who retired in 1964. Five years later Rowntrees merged with John Mackintosh & Sons, another Yorkshire-based company famous for its toffees which had its origins in a small pastrycook's shop opened in Halifax in 1890. Although Rowntree Mackintosh is no longer a family firm, it continues to be an enlightened employer. In front of the Haxby Road factory today is a free library for the use of the staff and across the road there is a theatre and swimming pool which is available for both employees and local residents. Inside the factory 5,800 people produce more than 80,000 tons of confectionery a year, including such popular brands as Kit-Kat, Smarties and Polos as well as the gums and pastilles which first got the company going.

The Rowntree trusts constitute one of the largest grant-making institutions in Britain today, having a combined capital of over £85 million. Among recent recipients of aid from the Charitable Trust are projects in the field of unemployment, peace groups in Northern Ireland and South Africa and Quaker service units. The latest list of grants by the Social Service Trust ranges alphabetically from the Aboriginal Commission to Europe to the Yorkshire Liberal Federation. In 1959 the Village Trust was transformed into the Joseph Rowntree Memorial Trust, an international research foundation with several practical responsibilities, particularly in the housing field. It has pioneered new leasehold arrangements for the elderly, shared ownership for first-time buyers and rented sheltered housing schemes.

New Earswick, which now has a population of just over 3,000, remains a model of good planning and a delight to walk around. The Folk Hall has been much extended since Joseph's time and is used for meetings of the village council, adult classes, opera club and camera club meetings and osteopathy clinics. It also houses religious services of the Roman Catholic and Elim Pentecostal

Churches, the Quakers, the Christadelphians and the Aga Kahn Community. In a referendum held in 1978, 87 per cent of the villagers voted in favour of allowing alcohol to be sold in the Folk Hall but strict rules lay down that it can only be served at functions run by the village council and that all profits must be used for local needs. Joseph Rowntree's wish that no one in the village should brew, store or sell alcohol for private gain is still respected.

9
JESSE BOOT
(1850–1931)

Ask anyone in a British High Street where the nearest big chemists is and the chances are that you will be directed to a branch of Boots. With over 1,000 shops across the country, as well as more than 200 overseas branches, Boots is to the retail pharmaceutical trade what Colmans is to mustard. It is also a major manufacturing company, producing chemicals, drugs, medical sundries and household goods. Today it employs over 68,000 people and ranks as the thirty-seventh largest firm in the United Kingdom. Yet when Jesse Boot launched the company a little over a hundred years ago it consisted of himself, his mother and sister, and two assistants working in a room 12 feet square. The spectacular growth of the business over the next forty years was almost entirely due to the energy, the flair and the relentless application of this one remarkable man.

Jesse Boot's career has many parallels with that of Thomas Holloway. Each lost his father when he was young and left school early to help in his mother's shop. Each made his fortune by brilliant advertising and forceful salesmanship in the booming market for medicines and cures in Victorian Britain. Each devoted the last years of his life to establishing a major educational institution to the construction of which he devoted meticulous care and attention. The two men shared a capacity for hard work and a preference for a simple lifestyle and there was in both their characters a strong strain of privacy which bordered on the secretive.

Jesse Boot was born in 1850 in Nottingham where his father, John, an agricultural labourer, had moved a year earlier to set up in business as a medical herbalist. His shop in Goosegate (so called because of its association with the traditional Goose Fair held annually in the city) was called the 'British and American Botanic Establishment' and advertised 'vegetable remedies'. Like many countrymen, John Boot had been brought up on folk remedies and as an active Methodist lay preacher he was almost certainly a devotee of John Wesley's *Primitive Physic, or an Easy and Natural Method of Curing Most Diseases*, in which the founder of Methodism had attacked the sophistication of the medical profession and brought together over 1,000 natural remedies. He was also a disciple of the Thomsonian theory which had originated in the United States and which held that all ills were produced by cold and could be treated by herbs which generated heat.

John Boot spent half his time out in the fields gathering herbs and the rest holding consultations in the back of his tiny shop. However, his own health broke down and in 1860 he died, leaving a widow, Mary, of thirty-four, a son, Jesse, of ten, and a daughter, Emily, of just eighteen months. Jesse was sent to the local grammar school but economic circumstances forced him to leave at thirteen so that he could help his mother in the shop. Together they trudged miles collecting herbs from hedgerows and meadows and going barefoot to preserve their leather boots for Sundays. The herbs were then dried and pulverized in the little back parlour where there was simple pill-making machinery of the kind that Thomas Holloway had used in his early days in London.

Jesse Boot was a solitary and serious-minded teenager. He inherited his father's strong religious principles and was a regular chapel-goer. This practice continued throughout his life although his denominational allegiance shifted from Wesleyan Methodist through Baptist and Congregationalist to Presbyterian. His religious sympathies, in fact, were very wide and encompassed both the Church of England, whose services he enjoyed, and the Salvation Army for which he had a particularly soft spot. William Booth, the Army's founder, had been a close friend of John Boot. Jesse also shared his father's love of singing. John Boot had died with the words of a Wesleyan hymn on his lips and as a young man Jesse sang in several chapel choirs.

In 1871 Jesse, now aged twenty-one, became a full partner in his mother's business. Realizing that herbal remedies were losing their appeal among an increasingly industrialized population, they had already begun to diversify and to stock patent proprietary medicines and some simple household goods. Alongside camomile, senna pods and liquorice, the shop sold soap, soda and candles and basic medicaments like Epsom salts, castor oil and camphor. For a time Jesse tried his hand as an itinerant salesman peddling patent medicines around local towns and villages. However, this did not prove profitable and in 1874 he decided to concentrate on retailing from the shop, buying in bulk and selling cheap. This decision was to prove the key to his subsequent success. He later recalled that the idea had come to him when he had been sent a hundredweight of Epsom salts from a debtor who was unable to pay him in cash. In an effort to shift the salts, Jesse, his mother and sister spent a weekend filling packets which they stacked in the shop window and priced at a penny a pound instead of the usual penny an ounce charged by other chemists. They found that they were very quickly sold out.

In the last year of his life Jesse Boot reflected on the reasons behind that first and all-important marketing decision:

> There was nothing very remarkable about my methods. They were simply the application of common sense. I found that everywhere articles, especially drugs, were being sold at ridiculously high prices, and were sold without any regard to neatness or attractiveness. My idea was simply to buy tons where others bought hundredweights or less, thus buying more cheaply, and making all the articles I sold look as attractive as possible.

Simple as it was, Boot's innovation was revolutionary. His price-cutting tactics directly challenged the well-established system of agreements between retail chemists which kept up the price of drugs and patent medicines. It was also unheard of for retailers to buy directly from manufacturers rather than through a wholesaler. This was to be a major feature of his strategy – as he later put it, 'the abolition of the middleman has been Boots' aim'. He made much of the fact that by buying direct from manufacturers and having a quick turnover his medicines were not only cheaper but also fresher than those of other chemists. Not surprisingly, his methods provoked considerable antagonism in the trade generally. For most of his life Boot was to be engaged in a spirited conflict against what he saw as the restrictive practices of traditional chemists. He was also to be the object of sustained campaigns from the Pharmaceutical Society to restrict his activities.

The initial decision to engage in price cutting was followed up by a major advertising campaign. With financial help from Nonconformist friends, Boot took large advertisements in the *Nottingham Daily Express* in February 1877 listing 128 patent medicines which were on sale at his shop at wholesale prices. Allen's Hair Restorer was cut from six shillings to three shillings and sixpence a bottle, Mother Siegel's syrup from two and six to one and ten, Woodward's Gripe Water from two and eight to one and ten, Woodhouse's Rheumatic Elixir was reduced by threepence a jar and Woodcock's wind pills by twopence a box. Also listed were certain own-name products like Boots' patent lobelia pills for asthma, indigestion and spasms and Boots' celebrated bronchial lozenges. The campaign was outstandingly successful. By April the shop was doing £40 of business a week (Jesse had calculated that he would break even on £20) and by May the weekly turnover was £100. Emboldened by the success, M.&J.Boot described itself variously in advertisements as 'The People's Store' and 'The Trade Reformer' and skilfully capitalized on a popular political movement by declaring its adherence to 'free trade and no monopoly'. By August the small shop had become the largest patent medicine dealer in Nottingham.

The principles which Jesse Boot introduced into his mother's shop in 1877 were to be the keynotes of his activities over the next forty years. Boots owed its success to a combination of extensive advertising and attractive display of goods, high turnover and small profit margins resulting from bulk buying and aggressive price cutting and the steady development of manufacturing and own-brand lines. Jesse Boot had no consuming interest in the products that he was making and selling. He did not share his father's enthusiasm for herbal medicine and he had no great knowledge of pharmacy. He was first and foremost a salesman with a passionate drive, almost amounting to a mission, to supply patent medicines and drugs to the new working-class market opening up in the cities of Britain in the aftermath of the Industrial Revolution. He was determined to become the biggest as well as the cheapest cash chemist in the country.

The immediate consequence of the price cutting and the advertising campaign of 1877 was a move by M.&J.Boot the following year into larger premises at no.18 Goosegate. Here for the first time the shop carried Jesse's name alone, with a notice across the top of the window proclaiming 'Drugs and Proprietary Articles at Reduced Prices'. On the ground floor were the shop, a small workshop where pills and ointments were made, an office and a store room. The first floor had stockrooms and the second floor, where Jesse and his mother lived, two bedrooms, two sitting rooms and a kitchen. In 1880 he bought the houses on either side of the shop to provide more space for manufacturing and the growing wholesale business. Three years later the three buildings were amalgamated to provide one enormous shop, with Jesse and his mother still living in modest rooms above. The shop front consisted of large plate-glass windows on both the ground and first floors divided by narrow twisted-iron columns which were painted in bright colours. The façade remains today and is still very striking although 16–18 Goosegate is now an arcade of small shops called Hockley Lanes.

Within the shop there were four distinct departments. Nearest the door was the grocery section which sold many articles normally found in a grocers, although not tea or coffee. Next to it was the patent medicines section, where the bulk of business was done, and opposite was the less popular herbs and sundries department which sold everything from surgical instruments to tooth brushes. Extending right across the back of the shop was the drugs counter and dispensary where doctors' prescriptions were made up by a qualified pharmacist. Boots' employment of a pharmacist was a source of considerable annoyance to rival establishments – not least because he charged half as much to dispense a prescription as they did – and was only possible after a High

Court judgement allowed the dispensing of medicines in departmental stores. Previously only those who had passed the qualifying examinations of the Pharmaceutical Society could legally keep shops at which drugs were on sale.

Boot used his extensive window space to mount spectacular displays of special lines and offers. One week he filled the windows with hops and another with sponges. In a typical and brilliant marketing gimmick on the day that the sixpenny telegram was introduced he wired 200 of the richest citizens of Nottingham inviting them to 'visit our exceptional display of sponges at Goosegate'. Instead of keeping customers waiting while their orders were weighed out, he had supplies of all popular lines weighed out in advance in a range of quantities. There was also a great stress on cleanliness. All the assistants wore clean white aprons and gloves. As well as dealing directly with customers who came into the shop, they also made up orders sent in from outlying villages which were collected by carriers. There was an extensive wholesale trade supplying smaller shops in the neighbourhood. On Saturdays the shop was open from eight in the morning until half past ten at night and attracted large numbers of farmers, visitors in town for the day and 'swell' shoppers who arrived in horse-drawn carriages, as well as the ordinary townsfolk who made up the bulk of Boots' customers.

There is no doubt that what drew people particularly to the shop in Goosegate were the special cut-price offers. G. R. Elliott, who started as an errand boy with Jesse Boot in 1881, has left a graphic description of these 'stunt' lines, as they were known:

An example was soft soap. The ordinary price was not less than 4d. per pound. Suddenly Mr Boot offered it at 4½d. for two pounds packed in a nice shapely parcel! The publicity would include, sometimes, a man or two men in the shop window weighing and wrapping the soap into parcels. Another line which made a sensation was tins of salmon. This was not a line which we had been stocking, but that didn't matter to Mr Boot. He evidently had the opportunity to buy a huge quantity advantageously, and took it. The usual price at that time was 8d.; Mr Boot's price was

4½d. per tin. Good quality too. After the news circulated, the sale was sensational. Many of the orders were 'a tin of salmon, please, and will you open it?' Tin openers were not to be found in every poor house then. It took a porter all his time to open fresh cases of tins for purchasers. Always, Mr Boot had something striking, something to make people talk about Boots.

During 1883 M. & J. Boot was reformed as a joint stock company with a capital of £4,698 subscribed by Jesse and his friends. By the end of the year Boot & Co. Ltd had a staff of nearly twenty under the control of a young general manager, Albert Thompson, who lived with Jesse and his mother above the shop. In 1884 branches were opened in Lincoln and Sheffield, both with qualified pharmacists. The following year a manufacturing department was established in a house adjoining the Goosegate shop. Initially it was on a very small scale, employing just one man, a Mr Holthouse, who made up the bronchial lozenges and lobelia pills which Mary Boot had previously turned out in her small back parlour. But from these modest beginnings a vast factory complex was to develop. Jesse Boot was not the first retail pharmacist to branch out into manufacturing – some years earlier Joseph Goddard had started making metal polish at his shop in nearby Leicester while in London T. H. W. Idris was making mineral waters – but he was to be easily the most successful.

The business took off rapidly. Annual sales increased from £5,000 in 1877 to £40,000 in 1885. Throughout this period Jesse Boot worked unceasingly. He started at seven in the morning, an hour before the shop opened, and when the shop closed at 9 p.m., he checked the stock and reordered, often working until eleven or later. On Saturdays the shop remained open until 10.30 p.m. Once there were several branches, Jesse worked right through the night once a fortnight on stocktaking. He had few recreations or diversions to relax and distract him. Throughout his life he forswore dancing, playing cards, going to the theatre or attending social occasions. As a young man he had sometimes allowed himself a glass of beer but for most of his life he was a complete teetotaller. He had few close friends. His only recreations were swimming

162

in the River Trent, taking long walks (he regularly walked the thirty-seven miles from Nottingham to Sheffield and also enjoyed solitary tramps in the Peak District) and cycling. He bought a tandem and spent many hours cycling with Albert Thompson.

Not surprisingly, Jesse Boot exhausted himself in his efforts to build up the firm and by October 1885 he had lost the will to continue and tried to sell the business. Unable to find a buyer, he suffered a breakdown in the early months of 1886. His sister suggested that he should take a holiday in the Channel Islands and he went to Jersey. There in the Methodist chapel in St Helier he met a twenty-three-year-old girl, Florence Rowe, the daughter of a local bookseller. They were married a few months later.

Marriage gave Boot a new lease of life and it also gave him a business partner who was to play a key role in the expansion of his company. Florence Boot came from a commercial family and took a very keen interest in her husband's business. For more than twenty years after their marriage she engaged all the shop and warehouse girls in Nottingham, supervised their welfare and toured branches settling industrial disputes. Every lunchtime she took their children to Jesse's office in Station Street, Nottingham, and, over food brought over from the nearby Midland Railway station, they discussed the firm's affairs. Florence had direct responsibility for what became known as the No. 2 department in the shops, covering gifts, fancy goods, stationery, artists' materials and books and it was largely thanks to her that this area was developed to provide an important and lucrative sideline to the main business in drugs and chemists' requisites.

In order to accommodate this new department the Goosegate shop was further extended in 1888 following a visit by Jesse Boot to the United States. A hydraulic passenger lift was installed and the first floor and basement were opened up as sales areas. The first floor was fitted out with a high-class dispensary and a counter selling expensive toiletries which was staffed by two 'superior' ladies. There was also an art department selling Winsor & Newton's paints and 'lots of articles of white wood designed for people to embellish with paint or enamel'. Later the floor also

163

housed departments selling stationery, books, fancy goods and Christmas cards. The basement was intended to be an iron-mongery department selling brushes, buckets, saucepans and doormats but, like the hydraulic lift which nervous customers refused to use, this did not prove a successful innovation and it was closed after less than two years. G.R.Elliott commented, 'It was one of the very few things which Mr Boot, having once taken hold of, relinquished'.

By now the number of shops bearing Boots' name was expanding rapidly. In 1887 the first branch outside the East Midlands was opened in Manchester. The following year the company changed its name to Boots Pure Drug Company Ltd. Subsidiary companies were later set up to cover operations in specific parts of the country, the first being Boots Cash Chemists (Lancashire) Ltd. By 1892 the number of branches had grown to 23, by 1894 to 45 and by 1897 to 126. By 1900 there were 180 covering every part of England except London and the Home Counties and the extreme North East. Boots was now twice as big as its nearest rival, Taylors Drug Stores (later to become Timothy Whites), which had been founded by another Wesleyan Methodist, W.B.Mason, who had opened his first cut-price chemist's shop in Leeds in 1886.

Jesse Boot took an immense interest in every detail of his shops. He was concerned with their design and appearance and took a particular pride in making new shops blend in with local archi-tectural styles, giving them Gothic or Tudor façades. In 1890 he established a shop-fitting department with a staff of thirty joiners, painters and designers. Good window space was regarded as parti-cularly important and along the top of every window was painted the distinctive Boots logo that is still used today. No one knows its origin, but it appeared on the Goosegate shop and was pre-sumably designed by Jesse himself, perhaps being derived from his signature. He made a habit of visiting all branches regularly, often travelling on horseback, and sometimes slept in a new shop the night before its opening to make sure that the first morning went smoothly. When a new branch was opened, he hired a brass band and up to twenty sandwich men to parade the streets while a tall Salvation Army man who worked in the packing department at Nottingham went round with a bell crying out the bargains to be had inside. This direct publicity was backed with extensive advertising in local newspapers.

Side by side with the expansion of the retail side of the business went the development of the manufacturing department. The prime purpose of this department was to supply the shops with their stock and as the number of branches increased so it outgrew its original Goosegate premises. In 1887 Boot took over a former lace and cotton factory in Island Street, Nottingham, just a few hundred yards from Samuel Morley's hosiery factories and warehouse. There in two great boiling pans medicines were mixed before being poured into bottles and stored ready for dispatch. Over the next ten years the factory was steadily enlarged and mechanized. Automatic equipment was introduced for washing, drying, filling and corking the medicine bottles. Steam-operated machinery for pill making was installed into which powder was fed at one end and tablets came out at the other. There were also machines for enclosing liquid drugs in capsules of flexible gelatine.

By 1893 the factory was employing 80 people and five years later the workforce was up to 542. There were now separate departments for the manufacture of pharmaceuticals, wet and dry chemicals, capsules, pills, soap, perfumes and mineral water. There were also extensive laboratories, packing and labelling rooms, stockrooms, a large counting-house and offices and a printing department equipped with five steam presses each capable of producing 10,000 circulars or handbills an hour. The Island Street works had its own carpenters' and plumbers' shops, a kitchen and mess room for all workers and a cart and waggon store complete with an extensive team of horses used for deliveries. It was conveniently sited near both the main Midland Railway line and the Trent canal up which barges brought bulk supplies of such essential raw materials as cod liver oil which was imported in large quantities from Norway.

The factory produced a wide range of those patent medicines and remedies which were so popular with the Victorians. In particular demand were chilli paste, a chest vapour made by squeezing chillies in a press; smelling salts made from ammonium carbonate crushed with a pestle and mortar; egg julep, a hair preparation which was a solution of soap and potassium carbonate in water; and Girards Glycerin, Cucumber and Honey Cream. The Island Street workforce had their own favourites among the products, notably Campbell's Cherry Cough Cure and Orange and Quinine Wine, both of which required alcohol in their manufacture, affording the opportunity for a surreptitious tipple if the manager wasn't looking. To encourage the expansion of manufacturing, Boots shop assistants were paid a commission on the sale of the company's own lines. Gradually more and more buildings were taken over in the area between the railway line and the canal and in 1914 a large purpose-built factory was erected in Island Street. By now Boots were producing forty-one different varieties of soap and several cosmetics as well as numerous medicines, and a total of 2,700 people were employed in the company's factories, warehouses and offices in Nottingham.

The retailing side also continued to expand in the early years of the twentieth century. In 1901 Boot bought out Day's Drug Stores, a chain of sixty-five chemists in London and the South East, for £113,000. Three years later he launched his first national advertising campaign, taking full-page advertisements in *The Times* and the *Daily Mail*. His choice of *The Times* was part of a deliberate policy to create a more up-market image for his shops. Another important element in this strategy was Florence Boot's establishment of Boots' Book Lovers' Library. Books for borrowing at twopence a title were put on shelves at the back of shops or upstairs so that those in search of them would have to walk through the main sales area and see the goods on display. In general the libraries were stocked with 'safe' novels, biographies and travel books. Slightly risqué or racy stories were marked out with a red label on the spine. By 1903, 193 branches of Boots had libraries and Jesse proudly claimed that they were 'extensively patronised by a thoughtful and cultured circle of customers'. A smaller number of shops also had tea rooms.

The spectacular growth of the Boots chain infuriated small retail chemists who objected to a limited liability company operating in a field which had hitherto been dominated by one-man businesses.

Both the Pharmaceutical Society and the more militant Proprietary Articles Trade Association fought on behalf of small chemists to secure a change in the law to prevent limited companies from engaging in the retail pharmaceutical trade and to enforce retail price maintenance but they were unsuccessful in their efforts. The 1906 Liberal Government came down firmly on the side of free trade. It also gave a significant boost to Boots' business when in 1913 it reserved the dispensing of medicines to qualified pharmacists. Hitherto doctors had dispensed about 90 per cent of their prescriptions themselves. Jesse Boot was delighted at the ending of this privilege for the medical profession. Like Thomas Holloway he held doctors in low regard, believing that they constituted an élitist priesthood who set out to confuse the public with their complicated Latin phrases and deliberate obscurity.

By 1914 there were 560 branches of Boots extending into Scotland as well as across England and Wales and with total takings of over £2.5 million. To the 'dissecting department' in Nottingham every Monday morning came the counterfoils of every purchase made in every shop during the previous week. By Tuesday Jesse knew exactly how many rhubarb pills had been sold in Liverpool or how much gripe water remained on the shelves at Plymouth. While he exercised a strong personal control over all aspects of the firm's development and took few, if any, into his confidence about future plans and projects, he delegated day-to-day matters to managers most of whom shared his own Nonconformist religious beliefs, puritanical attitudes and capacity for hard work. Prominent among them was Duncan Campbell who saw his most important function as being to save 'fallen' employees who had succumbed to some vice.

Jesse Boot's attitude to his workforce was autocratic but generally beneficent. He was much influenced by the writings on industrial relations of both George Cadbury and Joseph Rowntree and he went as far as buying a 35-acre estate on the outskirts of Nottingham with the idea of establishing there a model village for his workers along the lines of Bournville. However, illness forced him to give up the project. He was also inhibited by a constant fear that his business might collapse, which made him very cautious about introducing major welfare schemes and reforms and extremely secretive in all his affairs. He was genuinely interested in profit sharing but never fully implemented his ideas in his own factories, although he did introduce a limited scheme among managers in 1912. He also offered shares to customers but was disappointed when relatively few took up his offer.

Boot introduced a number of interesting and enlightened schemes to promote the welfare of his employees. Scholarships of £200 were offered to those who chose to study pharmacy, and later on all those between sixteen and twenty who worked in the firm's offices were encouraged to take a three-year commercial diploma course at University College, Nottingham. To encourage employees to take out life insurance, the company paid the first two annual premiums and half of all subsequent premiums. A pension fund for chemists was started in 1897 and later extended to the entire workforce. Sports grounds and a convalescent home were provided for factory workers and around 1900 Boot built a summer house, called the Plaisaunce, in a park on the south bank of the River Trent. Regular entertainments were laid on there for senior staff and all employees were invited on certain days every year. There were also regular works outings. Jesse himself led a visit to the Derbyshire hills in August 1894. The programme survives in the company archives. It has detailed descriptions of the geology and natural history of the area to be visited, precise instructions as to travel arrangements and ends with a stinging attack on the owner of Kinder Scout for refusing public access to its magnificent slopes. 'The mountainside should be as open to the wayfarer as the sea beach.'

Florence Boot continued to take a strong and active interest in the welfare of female employees. When she discovered that several of them did not get any breakfast she provided hot cocoa before the morning's work started. Like Caroline Colman, she took a particular interest in the girls' spiritual and moral development. Every Christmas she sent each one a silk banner printed with a verse from a hymn or a few lines of improving poetry. When girls left to get married, she presented them with a Bible. She laid on tea parties, concerts and sewing parties at the Plaisaunce. These occasions always concluded with the singing of a hymn, after which a fleet of horse-drawn buggies took the girls home. Florence Boot also organized special excursions for the female employees – in 1902 she took 500 girls to Skegness and in 1908 943 women staff went by special train to see the Franco-British Exhibition in London. In 1911 Eleanor Kelly, who had formerly worked at Bournville, was appointed as a welfare worker among the girls. She opened a sick room and visited those who were ill. Later a full-scale welfare department was set up catering for both male and female employees and a local doctor visited the factory two or three times a week.

Although nearly all of Jesse Boot's time was taken up with the affairs of his company, he was also involved in several philanthropic projects in the town of Nottingham. In 1908 he established eleven homes, in memory of his elder daughter Dorothy, for veterans of the Crimean War and the Indian Mutiny. In the same year he contributed the bulk of the money needed to rebuild Albert Hall, a centre for temperance meetings and Wesleyan Methodist services in the town. He also gave £5,000 for the construction of an organ in the hall on condition that popular recitals would be held there every Saturday afternoon with 'a fair number of seats at a charge not exceeding 3d each'. In 1984 the Methodists sold the hall and it has now been turned into a night club, but Boot's organ remains.

Jesse Boot was a staunch Liberal in politics and contributed much to the party's coffers. His brand of Liberalism can be deduced from the fact that he paid the campaigning expenses of Arthur Richardson, a free trader with labour leanings who stood against a Liberal Unionist in Nottingham in the 1906 and 1910 elections. Largely for his services to the Liberal Party Boot was knighted in 1909 and received a baronetcy in 1916. The following year he acquired a controlling interest in an ailing Liberal local paper, the *Nottingham Daily Express*, which he later sold to Rowntree's Westminster Press group. From 1910 to 1931 Boot was President of the Nottingham Liberal Association. He was a friend of the Liberal premier, H.H.Asquith, but generally shunned political and social gatherings and continued to lead a quiet life even when he had considerable wealth. Friends were amazed that he did not buy a car until 1904.

The First World War saw a considerable expansion in the manufacturing side of Boots. New products were introduced for the troops in the trenches, like water sterilizers, vermin powder, pocket air pillows, pocket stoves and box respirators to be worn at times of poison gas attacks. Encouraged by the government, the company also began large-scale production of synthetic drugs which had hitherto been chiefly supplied from Germany, among them aspirin, phenacetin and saccharin. In the first three years of the war the total number of Boots employees increased from 9,343 to 12,339.

By the end of the war Jesse Boot had decided to sell his company, the assets of which were now approaching £7 million. This was partly because of his own very poor state of health. Until his late forties he had been a strong and vigorous man who took a lot of exercise, but around 1900 he began to develop rheumatoid arthritis. Spa treatment at Buxton and exercise on a tricycle failed to stem the spread of the disease and by 1908 he was confined to a wheelchair. By 1918 he was in virtually constant pain and almost totally paralysed, hardly being able to move his head or his hands. Not surprisingly, his progressive disability made him increasingly irritable and bad-tempered.

The obvious person to succeed Jesse Boot in the family business was his son, John. But he was the antithesis of all that his father stood for and Jesse was determined that he should not take over the firm. John Boot loved drinking, dancing and the theatre. After a day in the office in Nottingham he would slip away to London for a party or a show and return by mail train early the following morning. Jesse tried to put a stop to these trips by insisting that his son was at his house every morning at eight to open the post. He also embarrassed John and his Cambridge friends considerably by holding his twenty-first birthday party at a Primitive Methodist chapel. Jesse was prepared to part with the company that he had created rather than see it run by someone whom he regarded as a profligate. He also had a more honourable motive in seeking to sell the business. Like Thomas Holloway, he wanted to spend his last years using the proceeds of his lifetime's work on some great philanthropic project.

Boot had first tried to sell his company in 1917 when he offered it to the American tycoon, H.G. Selfridge, for the ridiculously low figure of £250,000. In 1920 he succeeded in selling it to another American, Louis Liggett, for the more realistic price of £2,274,600. Liggett was a man very much in the same mould as Jesse Boot. A poor boy who had started out as a patent medicine vendor, he had built up a business on the basis of hard-selling a tonic made from cod liver oil and sherry; in this way he had become head of the Rexall Group which dominated the retail pharmaceutical trade in the United States in much the same way that Boots did in Britain. Both Jesse Boot's employees and his family were infuriated when they heard of the deal which he had kept completely to himself. Liggett too was less than happy when he found that the company he had taken over had a number of problems, including overstocking, low profits and heavy debts to banks. To the intense annoyance of Jesse, he made John Boot a director to provide continuity and help smooth some of the ruffled feathers.

For the last ten years of his life Jesse Boot devoted himself as far as his considerable disability would allow to his great philanthropic project. He retired to Jersey and also bought a villa near Cannes in the south of France but his heart remained in his native Nottingham where he was determined to leave a lasting and substantial memorial. He began by spending £250,000 on a park on the banks of the Trent, giving substantial sums to local hospitals and endowing a chair of sociology at the local Congregational college. He also set about planning what was to be his major contribution to the town, the provision of buildings and facilities which would enable the University College established there in 1881 to become a fully-fledged university.

As a site for the new university Boot provided the 35-acre Highfields estate which he had originally earmarked for a model industrial village. He was determined that this magnificent wooded park, which overlooked the Trent, should be used by the ordinary townsfolk of Nottingham as well as the students who would come to study there. A wide boulevard was built to link Highfields with the town centre and a public park was created in the southern part of the estate complete with boating lake, playing fields and the largest open-air swimming pool in the country. To design the university buildings Boot employed Morley Horder, the architect who had designed the façades for many of his shops. He himself took complete charge of the entire building project and would not even allow the principal or staff of the existing University College on to the site during construction work. Altogether he spent well over £1 million, providing not just buildings but also equipment and furniture for the new educational establishment.

The new University College (Nottingham did not, in fact, become a full university in its own right until twenty years later) was opened by King George V and Queen Mary in 1928. Boot was too ill to be present at the ceremony but it was relayed to him in a private room and the king and queen took tea with him afterwards. A few months later he was elevated to the peerage and took the title Lord Trent of Nottingham. Increasingly infirm and racked with pain, he died in 1931.

Jesse Boot did not win the same love and affection from his employees and those around him as George Cadbury or Joseph Rowntree. This was not because he lived a life of luxury that distanced himself from them – far from it, for as we have seen his tastes were simple, almost puritanical, and his pleasures few. It was rather because of the reserved, almost secretive, nature of his character and the coldness which he tended to show to others, particularly as his illness tightened its terrible grip on him. Boot was stern on himself and he could be stern towards his subordinates. He believed that people should pull themselves up by their own effort, as he himself had, and was perhaps slightly lacking in sympathy for the weaker and frailer brethren. But at the same time he was capable of spontaneous acts of great generosity and his evident deep faith and strength of character won the respect, and perhaps the awe, of many of his employees. In the words of G.R. Elliott, 'As a clean-living, clear-thinking man, Mr Boot would have been hard to equal'.

Two years after Jesse Boot's death his company came back into

British ownership when the American United Drug Company went bankrupt. John Boot, now the second Lord Trent, became chairman and managing director. One of his first acts was to open a new factory complex at Beeston, just across the river from the Highfields estate. The following year he unveiled a bronze bust of his father in front of the University College buildings. The inscription on the base reads: 'Our great citizen, Jesse Boot, Lord Trent. Before him lies the monument of his industry; behind, an everlasting monument of his benevolence.' D. H. Lawrence, another famous son of Nottingham, provided a simpler epitaph in one of his poems:

> In Nottingham, that dismal town
> where I went to school and college,
> they've built a new university
> for a new dispensation of knowledge.
>
> Built it most grand and cakeily
> out of the noble loot
> derived from shrewd cash-chemistry
> by good Sir Jesse Boot.

10
WILLIAM HESKETH LEVER
(1851–1925)

One of the distinguishing features of the true entrepreneur is surely that he spots and seizes opportunities which the rest of us would either miss or fail to take, whether through fear, lack of imagination or laziness. If Titus Salt had not experimented with the contents of the dirty-looking bales he saw lying in the docks at Liverpool in 1834, and which others had written off as useless, the mighty mill at Saltaire, and with it much of the West Yorkshire worsted industry, would never have come into existence. Similarly if George Cadbury had not recognized the significance of the new Dutch cocoa press in 1866 and been determined to introduce it into Britain, his name would probably now be forgotten instead of being found on wrappers on every supermarket shelf and corner shop counter.

William Lever traced the origins of his fortunes to a much smaller decision which he took one afternoon in 1877 when he was a young commercial traveller for his father's wholesale grocery business in Lancashire. For once he had finished the day's calls early – at half-past three. A lazier and weaker soul would have been tempted to call it a day and head his horse and trap for home. But not so Lever. He pressed on to a village which had hitherto been outside the firm's catchment area and there he secured half a dozen orders for eggs, butter and soap. On subsequent visits to the area, he gradually pushed further and further into this unknown territory until he was eventually so far from base that his father told him to set up his own branch of the business to serve the new area. Free to develop his flair for marketing and publicity, Lever began to concentrate on the sale of soap, for which he saw there was a

strong demand among the housewives of this heavily industrialized and polluted part of the country. Five years later he set
up a small soap-manufacturing company.

The firm which developed from that decision to prolong an afternoon's work is now the largest producer of consumer goods in the
world. Unilever, formed four years after Lever's death as the
result of a merger between his own companies and a number of
Dutch-based firms, is the thirtieth biggest industrial grouping in
the world and the seventh highest profit maker in the United
Kingdom. It is on a scale vastly greater than any of the other
companies featured in this book. Yet its origins are remarkably
similar to theirs, and its founder was a man who in every respect
fits into the mould of an enlightened Victorian entrepreneur. In
many ways, indeed, he represents the last of the line and is a
wholly fitting subject for the final chapter.

Lever lacked the commanding physical presence and the Old
Testamental appearance of many of the great Victorian Nonconformist industrialists. But what he lacked in physical stature he
more than made up for in drive and energy. A contemporary described him thus: 'Short and thickset in stature with a sturdy body
set on short legs and a massive head covered with thick, upstand-
ing hair, he radiated force and energy.' A consummate salesman,
he effectively pioneered the techniques of mass marketing in
Britain, working partly on the basis of native intuition and a careful study of the demands of the growing body of working-class
consumers and partly on the basis of applying lessons learned in
the United States. He was also a politician and philanthropist of
considerable vision many of whose ideas have much relevance
today.

Appropriately for a man who came to epitomize Britain's industrial and commercial pre-eminence in the latter part of the nineteenth century, William Hesketh Lever was born in 1851, the year
of the Great Exhibition at the Crystal Palace, and in that part of
the country which perhaps more than any other was the power-
house of the workshop of the world. His birthplace, Bolton, was in
the heart of the Lancashire cotton industry where hundreds of
mills produced the material which was Britain's biggest export for

much of Queen Victoria's reign. William and his nine brothers and sisters were brought up strictly. Their father, James Lever, was a devout Congregationalist who banned smoking and drinking in the house and read the Bible aloud to the family every morning. On Sundays the children attended not just morning and evening service at the local Congregational chapel, but early morning and afternoon Sunday School as well. Lever was never to show any resentment over this stern childhood regime. Quite the contrary, in fact. He remained a strong Congregationalist throughout his life and himself became a Sunday School superintendent.

Like both Titus Salt and George Cadbury, Lever originally wanted to become a doctor and his mother backed him in this choice of career. The demands of the family business called, however, and at fifteen he left school to become apprenticed to the grocery firm of which his father was a partner. At that time there were about twenty-five people working for the firm. William certainly did not get preferential treatment as the son of one of the bosses. His pay was just one shilling a week and for this he was expected to be up at seven in the morning to sweep out the shop and take down the shutters before a full day's work cutting up the long bars of soap which arrived from the manufacturers, breaking up the equally large loaves of sugar from the refiners and stacking up orders on a hand trolley and wheeling them out to the carts of the local retailers. Notwithstanding this demanding life, he found time in the evenings to learn shorthand and French, to read voraciously, particularly from the Bible and the works of Dickens and Shakespeare, and to enjoy walking and swimming.

At the age of nineteen William was made a commercial traveller, a position which he was to occupy in the firm for the next ten years. At the age of twenty-one he became a partner in the business with a salary of £800 a year. Thus financially provided, he felt able to propose to the girl who had for many years been his sweetheart, Elizabeth Hulme, the daughter of a Bolton linen draper who was also a staunch Congregationalist. The couple married in 1874.

William's success in winning new orders in outlying villages in 1877 led to him setting up his own branch of the business in Wigan.

Determined to get direct access to the main sources of supply and cut out middlemen, he went to Ireland and appointed agents who would buy butter and eggs direct from farmers. He also set up packing and dispatch centres there to ensure that these perishable commodities reached his warehouse as quickly as possible. A keen carpenter, he even designed a new kind of egg crate which he had patented. He also advertised his butter locally and posters appeared extolling the virtues of Lever's 'Fresh Ulster Lumps'.

By 1884 Lever & Co. were the biggest wholesale grocers in the north-west of England outside the two big cities of Liverpool and Manchester. That summer William and Elizabeth took a holiday in the Highlands and Islands of Scotland. That wild and romantic part of Britain was to make a lasting impression on Lever. It very nearly inspired him there and then to give up business life at the age of only thirty-three. Hearing that one of the small islands in the Orkneys was for sale, he was very tempted to sell his share in the company and retire there. 'I never felt less inclined to return to business in my life', he later wrote. He resisted the temptation, however, and, like Jesse Boot two years later, he returned from his temporary island retreat with renewed commercial vigour and a determination to expand his business.

Specifically he decided that he would concentrate on selling one particular line and he resolved that it would be household soap. It was a shrewd judgement. The grime and pollution of Britain's new industrial towns and cities had greatly increased the need for more frequent washing of both clothes and bodies and for more powerful soaps to cope with the effects of smoke and oil. The soap trade had also been given a powerful boost by those twin gods of the Victorian Age – free trade and evangelical religion. As chancellor of the exchequer in 1853, W. E. Gladstone had removed the excise duty of threepence a pound on soap. In the next two decades total consumption of soap in Britain doubled from 100,000 to 200,000 tons a year, helped partly by the message of preachers and tracts that cleanliness was second only to godliness in the catalogue of Christian virtues. The influence of successive government public health Acts, growing concern about the role of dirt in spreading disease and the spread of public laundries and bath houses also helped to increase the demand for soap.

A shrewd calculation of the benefits to be reaped from supplying this growing market must surely have been at the basis of Lever's decision to concentrate on soap in 1884. He himself gave a more romantic and ingenuous explanation when asked many years later what had prompted the decision: 'Why I thought of soap more than anything else I do not know, except that the wrapping of soap was my first occupation when I went into the grocery business.' It is a nice thought and perhaps there is some truth in it. If Lever was, in fact, inspired to enter the soap trade by his early experiences, then he was not the first man to make a fortune out of revolutionizing a tedious chore that he had performed as a grocer's apprentice. In 1872 Henry Tate, who had worked as a boy in a shop just a few miles from Bolton, had patented a machine for cutting up loaves of sugar into small cubes for domestic use. Such was the beginning of the giant sugar firm of Tate & Lyle.

Until Lever entered the business and changed it, most soap in Britain was supplied in anonymous bars which were cut into lengths by grocers according to the weight required by their customers. Lever & Co. had themselves in 1874 started calling one of the soaps which they sold 'Lever's Pure Honey'. However, as it was neither pure nor made of honey, it fell foul of the provisions of the Sale of Food and Drugs Act passed the following year; nor could it be registered under the new Trade Marks Act. Lever recognized the critical importance of having a distinctive and appealing brand name for the high-quality soap which he wished to sell. He approached W.P.Thompson, a trade mark and patent agent in Liverpool, who put down a list of half a dozen possible names on a sheet of paper. At first none of them appealed to Lever and he went away with the list in his pocket, feeling disappointed. Every time he had a few minutes to spare he took out the list and studied it. Then suddenly it hit him that one of the names, Sunlight, was absolutely right and he rushed off to have it patented.

Sunlight Soap was destined to become a household name not just in Britain but right across the world. Lever prudently registered it in every country where the Trade Marks Act was in force. He also began to advertise it intensively, creating his own magazine, the *Lancashire Grocer*, to sing its praises among retailers, and signing contracts with the London North Western and Lancashire & Yorkshire Railway Companies to erect metal hoardings on their stations. On these signs the name Sunlight was embellished by a quotation from Shakespeare's *King Lear*, 'See how this becomes the house'. So began a major advertising campaign, in which the words of great writers and the paintings of great artists were to be employed, along with much doggerel and hyperbole, to sell a simple household soap.

When the Sunlight trade mark was introduced in 1884 it covered a variety of different soaps which were produced by a number of manufacturers for Lever & Co. and supplied to grocers from the firm's wholesale shops in Bolton and Wigan. One in particular caught William Lever's attention. It was a hard laundry soap made by the firm of Joseph Watson in Leeds which had remarkably good lathering properties. It was sold as Sunlight Self-Washer because, it was claimed, it would wash clothes by itself without the scrubbing, pounding and rubbing that was necessary with other soaps. The secret lay in the fact that it was made from vegetable oils rather than the more commonly used ingredient, tallow. This method of production had one severe drawback. The oils tended to go rancid and produce an evil smell. But despite this, it was clear to Lever that his customers liked it:

One day a customer walked into our warehouse at Wigan and said 'I want some more of that stinking soap'. Her customers, although the soap stank, came back for it because, of course, it was only rancid on the outside; you had just got to use the soap for a few times in your hands and this outer skin which had gone rancid was all washed away, and the soap underneath was as good and sweet and fresh as soap could possibly be. It was only the effect of the oxygen in the air which oxygenized the oil and made it rancid; the inside, if you cut a bar in two, was always perfect soap.

The discovery of what made Sunlight Soap go rancid led Lever to introduce what was almost certainly the greatest innovation in the British soap industry in the nineteenth century. To protect each tablet from oxygenization, he wrapped it in parchment paper. Later, borrowing a marketing idea from the United States, he introduced further packaging in the form of a brightly coloured printed carton. This served a double function – it preserved the appearance and scent of the soap and it kept the brand name before the buyer. In 1885 Sunlight became the first soap in Britain to be supplied to grocers ready cut into squares and wrapped. In the same year Lever took another momentous decision which was to have dramatic implications both for the British soap industry and for his own future. Dissatisfied with the quality achieved by Joseph Watson, he decided that he would do better making Sunlight soap himself. To the consternation of his father who sought in vain to persuade him that Levers should stick to the trade that they knew and not enter manufacturing, he raised capital of £27,000 and took a six-year lease on a soap factory in Warrington.

The first experimental boil of soap took place in October 1885 and by the following January the factory was producing 20 tons a week. Lever started by employing ten people, including Percy Winser, the works manager, and Edward Wainwright, the soap boiler, who had worked in the Warrington factory before he took it over. They perfected a formula for making Sunlight Self-Washer with maximum lathering properties and minimum smell which was based on using a carefully proportioned mix of copra or palm kernel oil, cotton seed oil, tallow and resin. Demand soon outstripped supply and Lever had to resort to putting curved iron rings round the top of the boiling pans to increase their capacity. By the end of 1887 production was up to 450 tons a week and Sunlight Self-Washer was selling better than any other soap in the United Kingdom.

This great success was attributable partly to the undoubted high quality of the soap itself. It was one of the first ever products to be subjected to rigorous quality control. Lever insisted that every batch was tested and he offered a £1,000 reward to anyone who could find any harmful additive. It was never claimed. Extremely careful marketing and inspired advertising also greatly boosted the sales of Sunlight. A large sales force was recruited and trained to check stocks in shops and to create striking window displays. They were also provided with a large amount of point-of-sale material, including counter signs, showcards and ceiling displays. The salesmen were exhorted to call at homes to demonstrate the superior washing powers of Sunlight and to carry out demonstrations in public places as well. The advertising campaign relied heavily on posters. One of the first and most successful showed a youth gazing at a placard which bore the question 'Why does a woman look old sooner than a man?' The answer, of course, lay in the fact that she tired herself out doing the washing, but needed to no longer thanks to the arrival of Sunlight Soap. Lever bought the slogan from an American soap maker, Frank Siddall of Philadelphia. He recalled later that in these early days he himself acted as advertising manager, sales manager and cashier rolled into one. It was a role which he relished. As soon as he had conquered one part of the country, he moved to another and when the whole of Britain was covered with Sunlight posters and hoardings, he moved overseas.

The Warrington factory had to be expanded considerably to cope with the growth in demand. The landlords of the site were unhelpful and refused to give permission for an extension. Undaunted, Lever went ahead and put up new buildings. 'I had to do so,' he said. 'To think of all those orders pouring in and having no soap.' But it rapidly became clear that even with the new buildings, the Warrington works would be inadequate. Lever resolved to find a new site. He realized his share in the family grocery business and set out with a local architect, William Owen, to explore the banks of the River Mersey. Before long they came across an area on the southern side of the river, about seven miles from Liverpool, five miles from Birkenhead and very close to Bromborough Pool where the model village for Price's Candle workers had been established in 1853. At first sight, it seemed an unpromising location for a new factory – it was an area of flat marshy fields traversed by creeks. But it had the great advantage of being very close to both the river and the railway line from Birkenhead to Chester. Bromborough Pool was far enough up the Mersey to be out of reach of the Liverpool Dock and Harbour dues yet deep enough to provide an anchorage where sea-going ships could transfer their cargoes to barges which could then travel to the factory wharves. The proximity of the river also meant that Lever could drive a hard bargain with the railway companies by threatening to transfer the distribution of his soap to coasters if they tried to charge too much.

Towards the end of 1887 Lever bought 56 acres of this land and building work started on the new factory which he decided to name Port Sunlight. Production at the new works began in January 1889 and in the first full year 16,000 tons of soap were manufactured. This output was achieved with the help of several technological innovations. Bigger pans were introduced which were heated by open steam coils and waste heat was recovered from the condensers. Another breakthrough was the recovery and sale of the glycerine which was produced during soap boiling. Although he had no technical expertise, Lever took a keen interest in all that was going on and closely supervised the running of the factory. He arrived there every morning at half-past eight carrying a concertina-like brown bag and went to his glass-walled office which had been specially built above the level of the main offices, rather like the bridge of a ship. Known as 'the chief', he ruled his staff in a highly autocratic way, dismissing two chemists for disclosing information to a member of the factory staff and even hiring a private detective to spy on a manager whom he believed to be slacking.

With output rising by 3,000 to 5,000 tons every year, it was not long before the Port Sunlight works had to be extended as Warrington had been before. In order to finance the development, the firm was in 1890 converted into a private limited company with an authorized capital of £300,000. Lever himself held most of the shares in what now became known as Lever Brothers Ltd. His brother, James D'Arcy Lever, very much took a back seat, and resigned through ill health in 1897. In 1894 Lever Brothers became a public company with a commencing capital of £1,500,000. The ordinary shares were held by William, who became chairman, with his brother, his father and P.J.Winser as directors. The initial issue of preference shares was greatly oversubscribed, as were all subsequent share issues. By 1896 Port Sunlight had its own mill to produce the oil needed for soap manufacture. Cattle cake was made from the crushed seeds and kernels. In his first ten years as a soap producer, Lever had increased his annual output from just under 3,000 to over 40,000 tons.

Not all of this was Sunlight Self-Washer. In 1894 Lever Brothers introduced another brand that was to become popular, Lifebuoy. This had the advantage of being made from the oil left over after the manufacture of Sunlight. It had a dark brown appearance and with the addition of carbolic acid it was marketed as a powerful germicide. Five years later Lever bought out an American soap maker, Benjamin Brooke of Philadelphia, who produced a scouring soap called Monkey Brand which was advertised with the slogan 'Won't wash clothes'. At the same time he first put soap flakes on the market. The first flakes, which were for toilet use, were not a great success but when in 1900 he introduced Lux flakes for the safe washing of woollens a new brand leader was established. Four years later Lever Brothers launched an equally successful scouring powder called Vim.

All of these new products were promoted with massive advertising campaigns. Altogether Lever spent an unprecedented £2 million on advertising in his first twenty years as a soap maker. The great bulk of this was spent on the product which continued to be the staple of the company's operations. The advertising for Sunlight Soap was aimed particularly at working-class housewives and involved much practical information. A book written by Lever himself and entitled *Sunlight Soap and How to Use It* was distributed to thousands of homes. Another publication, *The Sunlight Year Book* was sent to teachers in elementary schools throughout the country. The famous Sunlight posters stressed the relief of drudgery and also had a strong patriotic flavour. A poster of 1889 featured Britannia showing the Port Sunlight works to the great American showman, P.T.Barnum, and pointing them out as 'the greatest show on earth'. The caption underneath ran 'Sunlight Soap – the source of England's cleanliness and comfort'.

Although they were primarily aimed at a working-class market, many of Lever Brothers' early advertisements had a distinctly cultural flavour. There was much use of quotations from Shakespeare and from other major British poets. Soon after Gilbert and Sullivan's popular operetta *The Mikado* first appeared in 1886, the company produced a series of parodies of its best-loved songs, all extolling the virtues of Sunlight Soap. 'Three little maids from school' was turned into this 'trio of Sunlight Soap Tablets':

> Three little aids to health are we,
> Powerful aids in tablets three,
> Harbingers all of purity,
> Three little aids to health!
> Everyone will our virtues own,
> Everywhere is our value known,
> Everything that is foul has flown
> From three little aids to health!

Not content with adapting the work of the country's best known song-writing team to suit his commercial purposes, Lever also cheerfully turned the paintings of leading contemporary artists into advertisements. At the Royal Academy Exhibition of 1889 he bought for £157 a painting by W. P. Frith which was entitled *The New Frock* and showed a small girl turning up a white pinafore for inspection. A few months later it appeared on poster sites around the country retitled *So Clean* and with the words 'Sunlight Soap' emblazoned across the top. Frith was not amused but Lever could at least point to the fact that he was not the first soap maker to use works of art in this way. Three years earlier Thomas Barratt had bought John Millais's painting *Bubbles* to use as an advertisement for Pears' Soap. Lever argued with some justification that his policy of using paintings to advertise Sunlight Soap spread the fame of contemporary artists and caused their work to be seen much more widely than would normally be the case. But it is hardly surprising that he did not endear himself to the art world. In 1892 he bought a painting by Bacon called *Wedding Morning* and commented 'It is only a moderate picture but very suitable for soap advertisement'.

As other manufacturers moved into the lucrative soap market and competition increased, Lever resorted to bolder tactics to increase his sales. He introduced prize schemes, at first confined to charitable purposes but later involving direct gifts to customers. All those who bought Sunlight Soap were asked to vote on which charity should receive a £2,000 prize. In 1887 a new boat was provided for the Royal National Lifeboat Institution as a result. A cash prize was introduced for the person who most nearly guessed the number of votes given to the winning charity and later on free gifts were offered to those who collected a certain number of wrappers. One customer collected 25,000 wrappers to win a motor car and eleven bicycles.

Other manufacturers complained about the ethics of these American-style promotion schemes and objected to the amount that Lever spent on advertising. But he was an unrepentant evangelist for publicity and promotion and sought to convince more sceptical colleagues of the benefits of a large advertising budget. He once converted a fellow-manufacturer who told him that he never purchased an advertised article if he could help it by asking him which mustard he asked for when he went into a shop. 'Why, Colmans of course', was the reply. 'There aren't any others, are there?' For Lever this response illustrated perfectly the power of advertising. As he characteristically put it:

> The man who whispers down a well
> About the goods he has to sell
> Will not make as many dollars
> As the man who climbs the tree and hollers!

It did not take long for Lever to try his salesmanship overseas. In 1888, while he was waiting somewhat impatiently for the Port Sunlight works to be built, he sailed across to the United States to arrange for an agency in New York. The same year an agency was opened in Sydney, Australia, and the following year Lever went on a sales promotion tour of Western Europe, while in 1890 he journeyed to Canada. In 1892 he made the first of five round-the-world voyages prospecting for new markets and manufacturing sites. His strategy was to build up sales in a particular country by intensive advertising and then build a factory there when the level of demand justified local production. Europe was the first market to be developed in this way and Switzerland the first country to have its own Lever Brothers factory. Lever began his campaign there by organizing a washing competition, or Fête des Blanchisseuses, on the shores of Lake Geneva on Easter Monday 1889. All the washerwomen from the towns around the lake were invited and the success of the venture led to the establishment of an office in Lausanne and to the building of a factory at Olten nine years later. Agencies were also set up in Holland and France and factories at Mannheim in Germany (1900) and Brussels, Belgium (1905).

Further afield, Lever Brothers opened a New York office in 1895 and took over existing soap factories in Cambridge, Massachusetts, in 1897 and in Philadelphia in 1899. Being an ardent devotee of American methods of marketing, Lever was particularly keen to break into the transatlantic market and he visited the United States annually between 1894 and 1898. The British Empire was another important sales area and by 1900 the company had factories operating in Toronto, Canada, and Sydney, Australia, and had acquired land for a works near Cape Town in South Africa.

Considerable expansion was taking place back home at Port Sunlight too, both at the factory itself and in the model village that was growing up next to it. Lever had first expressed his desire to create such a community in a brief speech after his wife had cut the first sod on the site of the new factory in 1888:

It is my hope, and my brother's hope, some day to build houses in which our work-people will be able to live and be comfortable – semi-detached houses, with gardens back and front, in which they will be able to know more about the science of life than they can in a back slum, and in which they will learn that there is more enjoyment in life than in the mere going to and returning from work and looking forward to Saturday night to draw their wages.

By the end of 1888 William Owen had been instructed to prepare plans for twenty-eight cottages. Work on them began the following spring and the village was expanded as more money became available. Lever conceived the village of Port Sunlight very much as Titus Salt saw Saltaire, as a community where his workers would enjoy a healthy physical and social environment free from the moral and physical pollution of city life. He described his purpose as being 'to socialise and Christianise business relations and get back again in the office, factory and workshop to that close family brotherhood that existed in the good old days of hand labour'. Port Sunlight village was also to be an experiment in profit sharing:

If I were to follow the usual mode of profit-sharing, I would send my workmen and work girls to the cash office at the end of the year and say 'You are going to receive £8 each; you have earned this money: it belongs to you. Take it and make whatever use you like of your money'. Instead of that I told them: '£8 is soon spent, and it will not do you much good if you send it down your throats in the form of bottles of whisky, bags of sweets, or fat geese at Christmas. On the other hand, if you leave this money with me, I shall use it to provide for you everything which makes life pleasant – viz nice houses, comfortable homes, and healthy recreation.

Altogether 800 cottages were built at Port Sunlight between 1889 and 1914. Most conformed to one of two basic designs, the kitchen cottage and the parlour cottage, but they were finished and decorated in a wide range of styles. The predominant style in the village was half-timbered Tudor, but there was also much use of Flemish, German and French red brick and of pebbledash. The cottages were grouped around greens and open spaces and all had gardens. There was also a generous supply of allotments and of public buildings. One of these, a recreation and dining hall where male workers could either buy meals or have their own dinners heated, was called the Gladstone Hall. It was opened by the great Liberal statesman, who had long been a hero of Lever's, in 1891. At the opening ceremony Gladstone alluded to the gloomy prediction of Thomas Carlyle that cash payment would become the principal link between men. 'In this hall', he went on, 'I have found living proof that cash payment is not the only nexus between man and man.'

In 1900 a large building known as the Hulme Hall was opened in the village to provide women with the facilities that the men enjoyed in the Gladstone Hall. Girls could obtain a dinner of meat, potatoes and vegetables for twopence, tart for a penny and tea for a halfpenny. The walls of both canteens were hung with paintings from Lever's extensive private collection. Other amenities provided for the villagers included a cottage hospital, schools, a concert hall and an open-air swimming pool. A temperance hotel was opened in 1900. Two years later a referendum showed that 80 per cent of the villagers favoured it having a licence to sell intoxicating drinks. Lever, who was himself a virtual teetotaller, regretfully bowed to the wishes of the majority but insisted that there should be no sale of alcoholic drinks on a Sunday.

Considerable provision was made for the religious life of the villagers. In 1891 Lever instituted a series of sacred concerts and lectures at the Gladstone Hall on Sunday evenings. When he built the village school in 1896 he arranged for the central hall to have a chancel so that it could be used for worship. Two years later he established a Sunday School and he himself laid aside an hour every Sunday to talk to the children there. In 1902 work began on a church for Port Sunlight. The building, which opened two years later, reflects Lever's interdenominationalism and his love of the architecture and ritual of Anglicanism while maintaining his attachment to the democratic and doctrinal principles of Congregationalism. It is built in late Perpendicular Gothic style and has the appearance both inside and outside of an English parish church. Yet it is part of the Congregational family (now the United Reformed Church) and Lever insisted that the worship be interdenominational and based on a service book drawn up by a committee representing several different strains within the Christian tradition.

Port Sunlight became a model community in many senses. In the early 1900s infant mortality there was 70 in 1,000 compared to 140 in 1,000 in nearby Liverpool. As in Saltaire there was a very high level of participation in societies and cultural events. Lever Brothers paid a full-time musician to run musical activities in the church and the village. The inhabitants were also renowned for their morality and sobriety. A visitor in 1907 was impressed to find that there had been only one illegitimate birth that year and that the oldest inhabitant could recall only one elopement. He commented: 'Sedate and well-disciplined as he is, the Port Sunlighter must owe a great deal to the atmosphere of morality and piety that he drinks in at every breath.'

By 1906 Lever Brothers owned a total of 330 acres in the vicinity of Port Sunlight. The works with its railway sidings, wharves and docks took up 90 acres, the village, with a population of 3,500, occupied 140 acres and the remaining 100 acres were held in reserve for future development. The company, which employed more than 3,600 people, was now the biggest soap manufacturer in the United Kingdom and was well established in many overseas countries. Like Jesse Boot, Lever had incurred the hostility of many of his competitors by the aggressive way in which he had expanded his business. He had an uneasy relationship with the Soap Manufacturers' Association and generally eschewed combinations and cartels, preferring to act independently. In 1906, however, in response to rising raw materials costs and in a bid to end expensive advertising and promotion wars, he tried to establish a combine of soap firms. He was defeated in this purpose largely by Lord Northcliffe who feared a loss of valuable advertising in his newspapers and mounted a savage campaign against Lever Brothers. Some of his allegations were so personal that Lever was to launch a successful series of libel actions against Northcliffe's papers, beginning with the *Daily Mail*.

The enormous wealth and success which was now coming his way did not greatly change Lever's lifestyle or attitudes. It is true that he had forsaken his modest terraced house in Wigan in 1889 for a large country house in the village of Thornton Hough on the Wirral peninsula and just a few miles from Port Sunlight. But within his new home he continued to lead a simple and even spartan life. He had the manor completely rebuilt, transforming it from being neo-Gothic to neo-Elizabethan and adding a strange structure on the roof consisting of a glass canopy supported by stilts and with only minimal protection around the sides. This was his bedroom where he slept every night, regardless of the weather. He rose every morning at five and spent twenty minutes exercising with clubs in a small gymnasium at the top of the house before returning to his outdoor shelter for a cold bath. After a cup of tea he then settled to two hours of report reading and letter writing before breakfast at half past seven. One of the workmen engaged on rebuilding work at the manor was heard to remark to another, 'Fancy, Bill, a bloke getting £500 a week regular and sleeping on the roof'.

Lever continued this habit until the last years of his life. In other respects, his life was a model of moderation. He never went to bed later than 10.30 p.m. and often retired for the night at 9 p.m. He gave up smoking at the age of forty-five, never touched coffee or spirits and confined his drinking to a little light wine two or three times a year. His energy and capacity for work were formidable. He often kept three stenographers busy with his rapid dictation and he used long journeys to conduct interviews. Those with whom he wished to talk travelled in a second car and were transferred to his own vehicle at strategic points along the way. This energy extended into his private life. After marriage, he lived in thirteen different houses, every one of which he rebuilt or substantially altered.

Religion remained important to William Lever throughout his life, although it could not be said that his was a conventional faith. He read a portion of the Bible every day, perhaps as much for practical advice as for spiritual guidance, and once remarked 'If a businessman has not read the Book of Proverbs, I will never believe that he can be a true, careful, sound and cautious businessman'. He built several churches but preferred the ethical teachings of Christianity to its creeds. After a visit to Egypt he wrote, 'The money spent on missionary effort is worse than wasted: the same money spent in taking little children out of the gutters in England, feeding, clothing and educating them decently until they are fifteen, then putting them in respectable service or the Colonies would do 10,000 times more good'.

Lever practised the social gospel of Christianity in his own life. He was a substantial and generous benefactor to many charitable and philanthropic projects. He gave a good deal of money for redevelopment in his native town of Bolton and in his adopted home of Thornton Hough where he established model houses, a school, an orphanage, shops and a recreation ground. In 1900 he gave a large park to the city of Liverpool and in 1907 he used the money which he had won in his libel actions against Lord Northcliffe's newspapers to endow schools of town planning, tropical medicine and Russian studies at Liverpool University.

Although somewhat autocratic, Lever was also philanthropic in his dealings with his employees. The Port Sunlight factory was equipped with a surgery, cloakrooms and showers to which the girls were brought in batches during the firm's time. They were also supplied with free overalls which were washed once a week, and they were given a shorter working week than the male employees. The girls started at eight and left at five, while the men worked from 7.50 until 5.30. This was partly for reasons of propriety; as a visitor in 1909 observed, 'It would not be conducive for the 2,000 men and boys and the 1,600 girls to leave the works in a confused stream, particularly during the reaction following upon release from work'. Female employees received a company pension at sixty and men at sixty-five. There was a scheme to provide sick pay and a holiday club which provided members with a week's holiday on full pay each year. Staff excursions took place most years. There was a day visit by 1,900 to the Paris Exhibition in 1900 and five years later 2,000 went to see the International Exhibition in Brussels while another 1,500 preferred a day trip to Blackpool.

There was a family atmosphere and a distinctly paternalistic flavour in many of the social events at Port Sunlight. During the winter months the company arranged weekly dances in the auditorium in the village. Every girl employed at the works was

191

invited to two dances a year. Those under eighteen were provided with partners by the firm and older girls were allowed to submit the names of their prospective partners to a social committee who issued invitations if they deemed them suitable. Lever himself entertained many employees at his home in Thornton Hough. In 1909 his son's coming of age was celebrated by a great party in the auditorium at which he was presented with a silver casket which had been paid for by contributions from 6,000 of Lever Brothers' 10,000 employees around the world.

Perhaps the most intriguing scheme introduced for the benefit of the employees was the profit-sharing arrangements established in 1909. Lever had long been an advocate of a more equal distribution of wealth between capital and labour. 'No employer-capitalist with a true feeling of brotherhood', he wrote, 'can be entirely happy in the fullest sense in the enjoyment of wealth without feeling a strong sense of dissatisfaction with present industrial conditions and a strong desire to improve them so that the employee-workmen may be raised to a much higher level in social well-being.' The basis of the scheme that he introduced at Port Sunlight was the establishment of a Co-Partnership Trust which effectively made employees ordinary shareholders by issuing certificates which attracted an annual dividend calculated in proportion to the company's profits. To qualify for inclusion in the scheme, employees had to be over twenty-five and to have worked for Lever Brothers for at least five years. They also had to sign an undertaking that they would not 'waste time, labour, materials or money' in the discharge of their duties. Certificates could be cancelled in cases of 'neglect of duty, dishonesty, intemperance, immorality, wilful misconduct, flagrant inefficiency or disloyalty'. Initially just over 1,000 employees were made co-partners under this scheme.

In 1906 William Lever got the chance to air his views on co-partnership and other issues more widely when he was elected to Parliament. Not surprisingly for one of strong Nonconformist principles who had been reared in the free-trading atmosphere of Lancashire, he was a dedicated Liberal and had already stood a number of times as the party's candidate for Birkenhead. He took a characteristically high-minded attitude to campaigning, refusing to canvass his own workers and only using a public building in Port Sunlight for a political meeting if there was also to be a Tory meeting there to provide balance. Within a few days of his arrival in the Commons he put forward a radical plan for its rebuilding. Like many other industrialist MPs, he disliked the slow pace and antiquated atmosphere of Westminster and was an infrequent attender at debates. But he did make an important mark in 1907 when he introduced a private member's bill to provide state old age pensions payable through the Post Office and funded through an increase in income tax. The measure was subsequently taken over by the government and passed as part of the package of measures associated with Lloyd George's People's Budget. Lever also spoke on several occasions in favour of the payment of MPs and against the growing class polarization in the country. He retired from the Commons in 1910.

The early years of the twentieth century saw continued expansion of Lever Brothers' activities, particularly overseas. Determined to secure control of the raw materials needed for soap production, Lever established palm oil plantations in the Solomon Islands and a phosphate company in the Marshall Islands. In 1911 he bought 6 million acres of land in the Belgian Congo where he established coconut mills and palm oil estates and he also acquired extensive plantations in Nigeria. The programme of setting up factories abroad continued with new plants being opened at Lille in France in 1910, Durban in South Africa in 1911, Shanghai in China in 1912, Tori-Shindon in Japan in 1913 and Vlaardingen in Holland in 1915. In 1916 the company went into shipping with the acquisition of six ships to convey raw materials from West Africa to Liverpool.

Nearer home, Lever bought another 7,000 acres of land on the Wirral which included rich salt deposits. This enabled the company to manufacture its own soda ash, the raw material for the caustic soda boiled up with fats to produce soap. By 1913 Lever Brothers were making half the soap sold in Britain, and with the newly introduced Persil they also had the brand leader in the fast-growing washing powder market. Lever himself, made a baronet in 1913, was becoming one of the most famous figures in the country, and one of the richest, with a personal fortune of around £3 million. In 1913 he and his wife Elizabeth dined with King George V and Queen Mary. A few months later Elizabeth died. In her memory Lever decided to build a large art gallery at Port Sunlight devoted principally to the work of contemporary British artists, but also housing the collection of ceramics and *objets d'art* which he had built up since his early twenties. The foundation stone of the new gallery was laid by King George V during a royal visit to Port Sunlight in March 1914.

During the First World War Lever displayed both his great patriotism and his commercial acumen. On the outbreak of war he put up posters at Port Sunlight encouraging all able-bodied men to enlist at the Gladstone Hall which was turned into a recruiting office for the Cheshire Regiment. More than 700 immediately heeded the call and on the first Sunday in September, after a church service, they went off by train to Chester were Lever led their march through the city to the castle and formally handed them over to the commanding officer. Over 4,000 men from Port Sunlight served in the war. Those who died are commemorated by a particularly striking war memorial in the village which was unveiled in 1921 by a worker in the soap factory who lost his sight at the Battle of the Somme and a member of the London office staff awarded the VC for conspicuous bravery and devotion to duty in Palestine. Lever himself, though now in his mid-sixties, took an active role in the Birkenhead and District Volunteer Training Corps where he was drilled by one of his own office commissionaires. He also served on the national working party set up by his friend Lloyd George to control the sale and supply of liquor in military, naval and munition areas and became treasurer of the Star and Garter Homes for Disabled Servicemen.

The patriotic feelings engendered by the war offered a splendid opportunity for some heart-stirring advertisements for Sunlight Soap. Mothers and sweethearts were enjoined to 'include a tablet in your next parcel to the fleet or the front' and reminded that 'while such quality exists, victory is assured'. A poster showing a soldier standing in the trenches with his foot resting on a box of

Sunlight was headed 'The CLEANEST fighter in the world – the British Tommy'. Underneath ran the caption:

The clean, chivalrous fighting instincts of our gallant soldiers reflect the ideals of our business life. The same characteristics which stamp the British Tommy as the CLEANEST FIGHTER IN THE WORLD have won equal repute for British goods. SUNLIGHT SOAP is typically British. Tommy welcomes it in the trenches just as you welcome it at home.

The same commercial instinct which produced these appeals to British patriotism led to an attempt to keep in with the enemy. Dedicated salesman that he was, Lever saw no reason why he should stop supplying soap to the Germans just because Britain was at war with them:

It would make the Germans clean but it would not make them better fighters; they could not eat it, therefore it would not nourish them, in fact as fighting machines they would not be affected at all, and whilst we all know that soap may have a good effect on health I do not think that life in the trenches or the battlefield, notwithstanding constant washings, can be affected very much by the question of what soap is issued, whether good soap from England or poor soap from Germany.

The government was not to be moved by this ingenious argument, however, and Lever Brothers were ordered to cease supplying Germany and German-occupied countries. But if the company lost one important market because of the war, it also gained a new product. Because of the shortage of edible fats brought about by disruption of imports, the government requested Lever to go into the manufacture of margarine. It also asked him to step up production of glycerine at Port Sunlight since it was a vital material in the manufacture of explosives. By the end of the war Lever Brothers were the biggest margarine makers in the United Kingdom. For his help to the war effort Lever was raised to the peerage in 1917. He took the title of Lord Leverhulme of Bolton-le-Moors, so showing his devotion both to his late wife, Elizabeth Hulme, and to the town of his birth.

The immediate aftermath of the First World War saw Lever embark on two grand and visionary schemes which failed because of opposition from those whom they were designed to help. Both were inspired by a genuine belief in self-help but they were rejected as paternalistic and interfering by two very different but equally independent communities. Their failure must have led Lever to ponder, much as Thomas Holloway had done half a century earlier, that it was considerably easier to amass a fortune than to spend it in efforts to improve the lot of your fellow men.

The first project involved an object which one might have thought would have won almost universal commendation, the reduction of the standard working day to six hours. The problem lay in the compulsory activities which Lever wished to substitute for the two hours lost on the factory floor and in the new shift patterns which he proposed in order to accommodate the six-hour day. Foreseeing that greater leisure was coming to all, he proposed nothing less than a national scheme of compulsory self-improvement for everyone between the ages of fourteen and thirty. His idea was that up to the age of twenty-four, two hours each working day should be devoted to education and physical training and for the next six years the same period should be used for military training and national service. In this way, he argued, 'After 30 years of age the citizen would have completed his period of compulsory attendance under State Regulations and would be fully equipped by education and training for all the duties of citizenship, and might reasonably be trusted to make, as did St Paul, but in his own way, his own voluntary contribution to social advancement and betterment'.

Lever attempted to launch his scheme on an experimental basis at Port Sunlight. He arranged for all office staff under eighteen to attend evening classes at the company's expense and in 1917 set up a company staff college. However, the trade unions representing the employees opposed the principle of compulsory education for their members and specifically rejected the two-shift system (8 a.m. to 2 p.m. and 2 p.m. to 8 p.m.) that would be necessary to run the plant efficiently on the basis of a six-hour day for each worker. Defeated in his own company, Lever abandoned the attempt to convince the government and the country at large of the wisdom of his imaginative proposals.

His second post-war project got rather further and resulted in Lever Brothers moving into a major new area of manufacturing which it still occupies today. It arose from Lever's fascination with the remote Western islands of Scotland which dated from his visit in 1884. When the island of Lewis came on the market in 1917 he seized the opportunity of acquiring it and two years later he bought the adjoining island of Harris. He resolved to transform the economy of the islands by establishing a major fishing and fish-processing industry complete with ice-making plants and canning factories. Not being one to do things by halves, he began by buying up the best fishmongers' shops in towns throughout Britain to create a chain of retail outlets, named Macfisheries, to sell the catches from the islands. He also turned Lever Brothers into food manufacturers by acquiring a number of companies which included Walls, the famous makers of ice-cream and sausages. However, his plans to undertake extensive building and redevelopment work on the islands themselves were largely frustrated by the opposition of the local crofters who preferred to cling to their tenuous but independent existence. In the end Lever conceded defeat and abandoned his great project, granting the crofters freehold possession of the land which they farmed. The whole episode is chronicled in a very witty poem by Louis MacNeice entitled *The Ballad of Lord Leverhulme*.

Lever very nearly suffered a third and much more damaging disaster in 1920 when he all but bankrupted the company by buying the ailing Niger Company of West Africa for £8 million. But despite these setbacks, Lever Brothers continued to expand and prosper in the early 1920s. By buying out most of the last remaining private soap manufacturers, they gained control of around two-thirds of total soap production in Britain. More factories were opened overseas and in 1921 the company acknowledged its status as a leading multinational by moving its headquarters from Port Sunlight to London. Three years later Lever Brothers took over British Oil and Cake Mills, a conglomeration of seed-crushing mills and oil refineries.

Lever himself continued his close supervision of all aspects of the company's affairs. Driven by a constant and almost obsessive fear of financial ruin and collapse, he ruled the firm very much in the manner of an absolute monarch and was reluctant to share decision making. He very rarely held board meetings, preferring to deal directly with individual directors and managers, whose signed but undated notices of resignation he is said to have had locked up in his office safe. But if he could be tyrannical in his approach to senior staff and boardroom colleagues, he also showed a deep and continuing concern for the welfare of shop-floor and office workers. On his last visit to the Lever Brothers soap factory in Norway he was greeted by the chairman who proudly announced that sales had reached an all-time record. 'I've no doubt about that', came the chairman's brusque reply, 'but what about the staff lavatories I complained of when I was here a year ago.'

In March 1925 Lever returned from his last long trip abroad, a visit to his extensive plantations and settlements in the Congo. On the voyage home he was asked by the ship's captain to read the lesson at the Sunday service. He chose the passage in the second chapter of Ecclesiastes which ends: 'Then I looked on all the works that my hands had wrought, and on the labour that I had laboured to do; and, behold, all was vanity and vexation of spirit, and there was no profit under the sun.' Shortly after his return to England, he presided at the annual meeting of Lever Brothers in London. He announced that the number of shareholders now totalled 187,000, and that the workforce amounted to 60,000, with a further 25,000 native Africans employed in central Africa and 1,000 directors and managers of associated companies. More than 18,000 of the company's employees were members of the co-partnership scheme. Altogether the Lever Brothers' empire encompassed 282 firms spread across the globe with a total capital valuation of £130 million. No other company in the world had wider geographical ramifications or more extensive commercial operations. Lever made one more foreign trip, in April, when he went to Brussels to show a film of his African journey to King Albert and Crown Prince Leopold. A week or so later he went up to Bolton and spoke to the Sunday School pupils at the Congregational church which he had given to the town. It was to be his last public appearance. He caught a chill after returning to London on the night sleeper and died a few days later, on 7 May 1925.

Lever's body lay in state for several days in the art gallery at Port Sunlight which he had built in memory of his wife and which had been opened just three years before his own death. Built in a severe classical style, it has something of the atmosphere of a mausoleum, albeit a particularly colourful one inside, being crammed with one of the finest private collections of paintings and porcelain in the United Kingdom. At its opening Lever had said, 'What I want this and succeeding generations to know, as they look on this building and its treasures, is that they are the creation not of genius, but of hard, plodding work within the reach of all those who wish to make the necessary sacrifice'. The words could well stand as his epitaph.

In his will, Lever left a proportion of his shares in Lever Brothers upon trust and specified that the income from them should be used to support certain charities and to provide scholarships for the purposes of education and research. The Leverhulme Trust made its first grants in 1932 and is now one of the leading grant-making bodies in Britain, with an income of more than £5 million. It provides scholarships for study abroad and endows university fellowships in the fields of applied science, humanities, economics, medicine and industrial relations. The trust is just one of Lever's legacies to our present age. The company which he created, now greatly enlarged as Unilever, still manufactures detergents and edible fats in addition to many other consumer products. Active in seventy-five countries, it employs more than 320,000 people. In Britain it is the biggest producer of washing powders, fabric conditioners, toilet soaps, and scourers and bleaches with such household names as Persil, Vim, Lux, Omo and Surf, as well as Sunlight and Lifebuoy soaps, which roll off automated production lines at Port Sunlight and Warrington, the site of Lever's original works where the company now has its second factory complex.

Port Sunlight village also continues to thrive although it is no longer necessary to be an employee or pensioner of the company to live there. The village has about 3,000 inhabitants living in more than 900 houses and flats. A fascinating Heritage Centre was established in 1984 in the former village library. It includes many pictures and objects associated with Lever's life, including the primitive hand machine with which he used to cut up bars of soap in his father's shop. There is also a shop at which you can buy bars of Sunlight Soap in their original style of wrapper. Recumbent effigies of William Lever and his wife lie on a tomb in an open chapel at the west end of the village church and he is also commemorated by a marble obelisk outside the art gallery which is flanked by figures representing industry, humanity and the arts.

The life of William Hesketh Lever has occupied a longer chapter than those of the other enlightened entrepreneurs featured in this book not necessarily because its achievements were greater but because it sums up the distinctive qualities of that remarkable breed of men. In him that potent mixture of Nonconformist rigour, Liberal idealism, commercial acumen and generosity of spirit that made Victorian Britain one of the most economically successful and humane civilizations that the world has ever seen reached its zenith. More, perhaps, than any other individual he combined and exemplified those qualities which have cropped up again and again in these pages – the drive and energy to create and exploit new markets and make technical innovations, the keen grasp of the importance of advertising and packaging in an age of rising living standards and the emergence of a mass consumer market, the determination to improve the material and moral life of workers and to break down the barriers between capital and labour, the conviction that wealth should be spread and used for the good of the community rather than hoarded or spent on oneself, and the simple but awe-inspiring capacity for sheer hard work.

I suspect that of all those qualities Lever himself would have rated the last as the most important. If there was a secular gospel of which he, in company with all the other enlightened entrepreneurs, was a faithful and unwavering disciple, it was the doctrine of self-help as propounded in the famous book by Samuel Smiles which came second only to the Bible in its influence and authority in many nineteenth-century homes. Lever was given a copy of Smiles's book by his father on his sixteenth birthday. He re-read it many times in later life and often turned to particular passages for advice and inspiration. He made a habit of presenting a copy of the work to young men whom he met and who struck him as having enterprise and enthusiasm. One such copy which he gave to a boy in the last year of his life is now in the Heritage Centre at Port Sunlight. On the front page is inscribed: 'It is impossible for me to say how much I owe to the fact that in my early youth I obtained a copy of Smiles' *Self-Help.*'

Of the many axioms and exhortations contained in Smiles's work, there is perhaps one which applies particularly to those who have been the subject of this book. It is the passage which occurs at the beginning of his chapter on application and perseverance:

> The greatest results in life are usually attained by simple means, and the exercise of ordinary qualities. The common life of every day, with its cares, necessities and duties, affords ample opportunity for acquiring experience of the best kind; and its most beaten paths provide the true worker with abundant scope for effort and room for self-improvement. The road of human welfare lies along the old highway of steadfast well-doing; and they who are the most persistent, and work in the truest spirit, will usually be the most successful.

The enlightened entrepreneurs who created products and businesses which are still household words a hundred years on and who established an approach towards industrial relations that we still have much to learn from today were not geniuses in the conventional sense of the word. What marked them out was rather their dogged, almost superhuman, attachment to the exercise of those commonplace, even humdrum qualities like regularity, application and methodicalness which were commended by Smiles and reinforced by the dictates of the Nonconformist Conscience. In a sense their success arose from their extraordinary pursuit of the ordinary. When Lever addressed the students of Liverpool University in 1922 on the secret of success in business he offered no complex psychological or sociological explanations. 'The conduct of successful business', he told them, 'merely consists in doing things in a very simple way, doing them regularly and never neglecting to do them.'

201

Suggestions for Further Reading

Jack Reynolds, *The Great Paternalist: Titus Salt and the Growth of Nineteenth Century Bradford* (Temple Smith, 1983).
Jack Reynolds, *Saltaire: An Introduction to the Village of Sir Titus Salt* (Bradford Art Galleries and Museums, 1976).

Edwin Hodder, *The Life of Samuel Morley* (1887).
Clyde Binfield, *George Williams and the YMCA* (Heinemann, 1973).

T.A.B.Corley, *Quaker Enterprise in Biscuits: Huntley and Palmers of Reading 1822–1972* (Hutchinson, 1972).

Helen Colman, *Jeremiah James Colman. A Memoir* (privately published, 1905).
The Advertising Art of J & J Colman (Norwich School of Art, 1977).

Andrew Carnegie, My Own Story (new edn, Carnegie Dunfermline Trust, 1984).
Joseph Frazier Wall, *Andrew Carnegie* (Oxford University Press, New York, 1970).
Simon Goodenough, *The Greatest Good Fortune – Andrew Carnegie's Gift for Today* (Macdonald, 1985).

A.G.Gardiner, *Life of George Cadbury* (Cassell, 1923).
Walter Stranz, *George Cadbury* (Shire Publications, 1973).

Anne Vernon, *A Quaker Businessman. The Life of Joseph Rowntree 1836–1925* (new edn, Sessions of York, 1982).

Stanley Chapman, *Jesse Boot of Boots the Chemists* (Hodder & Stoughton, 1974).

Charles Wilson, *The History of Unilever*, volume 1 (Cassell, 1970).
W.P.Jolly, *Lord Leverhulme* (Constable, 1976).
Nigel Nicolson, *Lord of the Isles* (Weidenfeld & Nicolson, 1960).

All the entrepreneurs featured in this book are also covered by entries in the *Dictionary of Business Biography* (Butterworths, 1982–6).

INDEX